Angel[illegible] of Foligno

Angela of Foligno

Passionate Mystic of the Double Abyss

Paul Lachance, O.F.M. (ed.)

New City Press
Hyde Park, New York

Published in the United States by New City Press
202 Cardinal Rd., Hyde Park, NY 12538
www.newcitypress.com

Cover design by Durva Correia
Cover illustration: The Blessed Angela of Foligno. Milan, Biblioteca Trivulziana, ms. 150 fo.17

Library of Congress Cataloging-in-Publication Data:
Angela, of Foligno, 124?-1309.
[Liber de vera fidelium experientia. English. Selections]
Angela of Foligno : the passionate mystic of the double abyss / Paul Lachance (ed.).
p. cm.
ISBN-13: 978-1-56548-248-7 (alk. paper)
ISBN-10: 1-56548-248-4 (alk paper)
1. Mysticism--Catholic Church. I. Title: Passionate mystic of the double abyss. II. Lachance, Paul. III. Title
BV5082.3.A54213 2006
248--dc22 2006005487

Printed in the United States of America

To
my Franciscan brothers
who make my work, including this
anthology, possible;
and to Jane.

Table of Contents

Introduction

Over the past twenty years, at least in the English-speaking world, Angela of Foligno has been raised from relative obscurity to rank as an outstanding representative of the Franciscan and Christian mystical tradition. Aside from contemporary interest in mysticism and the feminist retrieval of the forgotten voices of women in the Christian tradition, recent initiatives have propelled Angela to contemporary awareness. They include a new critical edition of her writings; hotly disputed textual issues; several international congresses; a flurry of anthologies, books, essays and assorted references; cinematic, theatrical, and musical productions; a renewed attempt at her canonization; translation of her writings into all the major languages, including the widely distributed English edition of her writings in the prestigious Classics of Western Spirituality series published by Paulist Press.[1] Recently, the noted University of Chicago scholar Bernard McGinn, in the *Flowering of*

1. Excerpts from *Angela of Foligno: Complete Works*, from The Classics of Western Spirituality, translated with an introduction by Paul Lachance, O.F.M., ©1993 by Paul Lachance, O.F.M, Paulist Press, Inc., New York/Mahwah, N.J. Used with permission of Paulist Press (www.paulistpress.com). This volume provides an extensive overview of Angela's life and times, information concerning the composition of her

Mysticism, the third volume of his widely acclaimed history of Christian mysticism, crowned Angela as one of the "four female medieval evangelists," the other three being Marguerite Porete, Mechtilde of Magdeburg, and Hadewijch. "Female evangelist" because of the daring and innovative ways in which these mystics described their experiences of God — as one without intermediary — and the bold claim that, much like the biblical texts, the accounts of these experiences were divinely inspired.

What also seems to strike a chord in contemporary sensitivity is the scorching and completely feminine way in which Angela narrates her dramatic love affair with the "passionate suffering God-man...." The intensity of her account, flowing on every page like molten lava, has no match in Christian mystical literature. Thomas Merton, in a conference on Angela, speaks of her ("one of the wild mystics") quite pertinently: "This is the great truth about her life: In her, passion, instead of being sort of locked up behind doors and left in a closet, becomes completely devoted to God. Passion gets completely caught up in her love for God and in the giving of herself to God."

---

book, further development of her inner journey, and the main themes of her spirituality and influence, all documented with abundant footnotes: and where all unfootnoted references in this anthology are to be found. For a good interpretative essay that compares the issues addressed by Angela's text with contemporary feminist concerns along with a fresh translation of part of her text, see Angela of Foligo's *Memorial*. Translated by John Cirignano with an introduction, notes and an interpretative essay by Cristina Mazzoni (Cambridge: D. S. Brewer, 1999). I am also indebted to Kathryn Krug and Terry Kelley for the translation of Angela's text, and to Colette Wisnewski for editing and making useful suggestions to this anthology.

Who Is Angela of Foligno?

As with many medieval saints and mystics, very little is known about the external facts and the circumstances surrounding Angela's life and the people who accompany her story. The date of her death, 4 January 1309, is well documented but all the others — her birth, conversion, events that marked her life — are largely conjectural. Virtually all we know about her must be gleaned from what has been referred to as her *Book,* which has been divided into two main parts. The first part, called the *Memorial,* contains a description of the thirty steps that led her into the abyss of Trinitarian life. "The faithful one of Christ" — Angela's name is never mentioned — recounted this narrative of her inner life to her anonymous Franciscan confessor, known only as Bro. A., and to her companion, known only as M. Bro. A., served Angela as confessor and scribe, as well as protagonist in her communications with God. He translated into Latin what Angela who was unlettered, dictated to him in her Umbrian dialect. Despite repeated statements to the contrary, he and other unnamed scribes or subsequent copyists, may have organized and reworked the text. A hot debate continues concerning the extent of his (or their) contribution to the redaction of the *Memorial.* Recent analysis of the manuscript tradition concerning the genesis of the *Memorial* suggests that Bro. A., for all his limitations, acted most prudently, as if he indeed were in the presence of a holy text. The second part of Angela's Book, the *Instructions,* highlights Angela's role as a spiritual mother. It also contains her teachings in the form of letters, exhortations, summaries of her spirituality, further visionary accounts, a testament, and an epilogue. It is likely that Bro. A. redacted some of these, but most came from anonymous disciples.

The First Twenty Years

It seems that Angela was born in 1248 — twenty years or so after the death of Saint Francis, in 1226 — in Foligno, a small town some six miles from Assisi. The *Memorial* contains details which suggest that Angela had been married, had children, and before her conversion lived what seems to have been a well-to-do, conventional life — even if she considered it a very sinful one. She and her family resided close to the Church of Saint Francis, which was administered by the Franciscans. After the death of her husband, she came into possession of other pieces of property, from which she gradually detached herself. The text suggests that a room in her residence, perhaps a private chapel, contained a crucifix with a suffering, bleeding Christ at whose feet were represented Saint John and the Blessed Virgin. Angela must have spent hours praying before this crucifix. This same room probably also contained a lectionary, which Angela used to meditate on the Holy Scriptures.

What triggered Angela's mid-life conversion, in or near 1285, is not known. When she was approximately 37 years old, the first step of the *Memorial* tells us, "Christ's faithful one" feared "being damned to hell" and "wept bitterly." Several factors may have influenced her to begin reorienting her life: a sudden awareness of the shallowness of her life, past and present; the anxiety-ridden atmosphere, in which a sudden end of the world was anticipated; the turmoil that obliged popes to take refuge from Rome in Perugia, then Avignon; the almost constant wars between Foligno and Perugia; and earthquakes that devastated the region. The example and preaching of nearby or itinerant Franciscans also may have led Angela to reexamine her life. In addition, the example of Pietro Crisci, a local nobleman (mentioned in the text) who adopted a hermit's life of strict poverty, may have provided Angela with an important role model for the choices she was about to make.

Whatever the cause, it is significant that in the very early stages of her conversion she called upon the "blessed Francis," who had appeared to her in a dream, to find her a good confessor to whom she could unburden herself. The Poverello was to be a central source of inspiration for her journey. Her *Book* records several visions in which he appeared to her. As Angela indicates in one of the *Instructions*, he is the one who taught her how to "recollect herself" and "become truly poor." At one point he startles her with the declaration: "You are the only one born of me."

Prompted by the promise Saint Francis made to her in this dream, Angela proceeded the next morning to the nearby Church of Saint Francis to find a confessor. She did not find who she was looking for there, but by chance on her return she entered the church of San Feliciano, the cathedral of Foligno, where she heard a Franciscan preaching. This man, the chaplain of the bishop and a relative of hers, was the one she had been seeking. After a full confession to him Angela felt greatly relieved. It is likely that this same friar later served as her spiritual guide and scribe, thus playing a decisive role in the composition of the *Memorial.*

Liberated and invigorated by her "good confession," Angela began to make changes in her life, "a few steps at a time," in order to respond to the new calling she was dimly perceiving. In a condensed fashion, the first nineteen steps of the *Memorial,* spanning a period of about six years, describe Angela's entrance into the way of penance, a season of purification through abundant tears and suffering. Illumined and set ablaze by the fire and intensity of Christ's love for her as revealed through increasingly vivid and focused visions of his passion and crucifixion, Angela became more and more aware of the shallowness of her past life and the overflow of divine mercy. Gradually, bitter and shameful memories healed as she grew into the knowledge of self, which later becomes a central theme of her spirituality. At this stage of her journey Angela has one desire: to grow in amorous response to the love she was receiving from Christ by spending long hours in prayer before the crucifix, practicing severe penances, and aligning her life with Christ's, which she later refers to as the "Book of Life."

Following the example of her model, Saint Francis, Angela gradually stripped herself of all her possessions and took steps to become truly poor. Also, early in her conversion, as mentioned in the ninth step, her mother, husband and sons died in unknown circumstances. Their deaths brought her relief, for they "freed her," as she says, "to give her heart to Christ."

In the seventeenth step, Angela's faith and experience take a quantum leap. Her faith becomes "different from the one she had before." She also asserts that she had been "led" more decisively into a mystical consciousness of God's inward presence by meditating on the Scriptures and taking "such delight in God's favors" that "she forgot not only the world but even herself." As a result of these momentary but powerful absorptions into the divine life, Angela's psyche was strung to a high point of tension. Step eighteen recounts that whenever she heard God mentioned she would shriek; she could hardly bear to see paintings of the passion of Christ, which made her feverish and sick. Angela, wanting still more from God, was told that if she indeed did give up her few remaining possessions the Holy Trinity would enter into her.

The twentieth step records Angela's pivotal pilgrimage to Assisi in order, as she puts it, to "feel Christ's presence, receive the grace of observing well" the Rule of the Third Order of Saint Francis which she had recently promised to accept, and above all "become, and remain to the end, truly poor." This pilgrimage, a high point of her journey, includes the promise of the indwelling of the Trinity in her soul being fulfilled. Halfway to Assisi, Angela received a numinous experience of God that held her entranced until she reached the basilica of Saint

Francis. Once inside, the second time she had entered, she caught sight of the depiction in stained glass of Christ holding Saint Francis closely to himself, a window that still can be seen today. It left her stunned. After "gently" and "gradually" the rapture left her, Angela began to roll on the pavement at the entrance to the basilica shrieking: "Love still unknown, why? Why? Why?" Angela's companions, not knowing how to deal with her, went to warn the Franciscans living in the Sacro Convento nearby. One of the friars, possibly the same who had heard her confession earlier, came out to see what was happening. After Angela's hysteria had calmed, he enjoined her to leave Assisi and not return until he could ascertain whether this experience had come from God or, as he was inclined to believe, from an evil spirit that had taken hold of her.

Subsequently, this same friar was named to the Franciscan friary in Foligno. In the adjacent church of San Francesco he met Angela and asked her to explain her bizarre behavior in Assisi. He wanted to write down what she said so he could consult another "spiritual man" to help him decide if God or the devil had been at work in her. Bro. A., as he is called throughout the *Memorial*, was stupefied by the account of the "divine secrets" that "Christ's faithful one" told him. He acknowledged that he could grasp what he heard only partially, comparing himself "to a sieve or sifter which does not retain the precious and refined flour but only the most coarse." He intended to transcribe Angela's words as faithfully as possible, translating into Latin what Angela said in her Umbrian dialect, rereading it to her several times to make sure that he had understood her correctly. For her part, Angela often insisted that everything he wrote was true, but "it was dry and without savor" and did not convey the meaning she intended.

Pressed by Bro A. to tell him everything, Angela first describes nineteen steps she had observed to that point in herself. There were another eleven steps, but confused with the notes he had taken and unsure how to organize the remaining material, Bro. A. condensed them into seven, which he described as "supplementary." The experiences narrated in these steps are much more amplified and detailed than in the preceding twenty, but only their more salient features will be noted.

The Seven Supplementary Steps

The first supplementary step completes what Bro. A. had already begun to write in the twentieth step. It includes an account of the theophany that occurred on the way to Assisi, the hysterical episode in front of the stained glass window of the Basilica of Saint Francis in Assisi and the return to Foligno, as well as her companion's report that as she lay bedridden an aura seemed to emanate from Angela's breast. More importantly, this step provides details of what Angela had heard and felt during the pilgrimage to Assisi. Among other things, she had heard God speaking to her most tenderly, assuring her that he loved her "more than any woman in the valley"; that henceforth she was betrothed to him, would wear the ring of his love, and that he would never leave her. Furthermore, it was confirmed to Angela that the Trinity, "at once one, and a union of many" had indeed entered into her soul.

In this step Angela also narrates several visions, many of which took place during the celebration of the Eucharist. She saw in the host "a beauty which far surpasses the beauty of the sun." She was upset that after the elevation the priest lowered the host to the altar too quickly. These Eucharistic moments brought her such joy that she wished they "would last forever." Like many other medieval mystics, particularly the women, Angela associated her visions during the celebration of the Eucharist closely with those of Christ's passion. They provide an insight into the inherent numinosity of Christ's emptying process in the Incarnation.

As Angela narrates in the second supplementary step, the fire of God's love set ablaze "all the members of her body," leaving her "thrilled with the delights of his presence." To remove any doubts whether God indeed was manifesting himself to her in such a way, he gave her a sign within the depths of her soul by which she would "continuously feel God's presence" and be "burning with love for him." No one, she was further assured, can find an excuse for not being saved. One need only present his or her wounds to Christ, the divine doctor, and do exactly as he says.

The third supplementary step contains an extensive description and discussion, supported with several examples, concerning those legitimately invited to eat and drink at a special table with the Lord. In the background, at the time a debate had been going on among Franciscans to identify the truly legitimate sons of Francis. Among the examples that demonstrate God's capacity to transform the bitterness of suffering into sweetness — a very Franciscan topos — Angela provides one that is especially striking. On Holy Thursday she and her companion had gone to the hospital to "find Christ" among the lepers. Having washed one of them whose skin was in an advanced stage of decomposition, they both drank of the very water used to wash the leper. "Its taste is so sweet," she declared, that "it was as if they had received Holy Communion." A similar episode transpired in the life of Francis of Assisi, when he drank from the same cup as a leper. As he reports in his Testament, encounters with lepers provided the key to his conversion: "When I was in sin, it seemed too bitter for me to see lepers. And the Lord Himself led me among them and I showed mercy to them. And when I left them, what had seemed bitter to me was turned into sweetness of soul and body. And afterwards I delayed a little and left the world."[2] For Francis and subsequently for Angela, lepers were icons of divine revelation. Angela, however, by drinking the very water used to wash a leper, radicalizes Francis's gesture. Repugnant as this may seem to our contemporary sensitivities, the noted French psychoanalyst Julia Kristeva, referring explicitly to both Francis and Angela, observes that "this mystical familiarity with abjection is a fount of infinite *jouissance*."[3] Other Italian mystics performed similar excessive gestures. Catherine of Siena and Catherine of Genoa ate pus or fleas from sick bodies. However, Angela's sacramental analogy is unique.

So far, the steps of the *Memorial* have revealed how the love that Angela experienced while contemplating Christ on the cross transformed and widened her own capacities to return that love in its infinite and mystical dimensions. The more she penetrated and shared in the sufferings of the one she refers to as "the suffering God-man" and the more she entered into the "poverty" and "contempt" — "the triad poverty, suffering, and contempt" summed up her following of Christ" — that he had endured, the more the secrets of the divine plan were revealed to her, namely the excessive love hidden in the abysses of the Trinitarian life and manifested by the incarnation and the crucifixion of the Son of God.

In these supplementary steps, Angela's experience of the passion of Christ is not only exterior but becomes more and more interior, "from within" the event itself. For instance, in the fourth supplementary step, while gazing at the cross, Angela says that she "saw and felt that Christ was within her, embracing her soul with the very arms with which he was

2. *The Saint,* Francis of Assisi: Early Documents, vol. 1, ed. Regis J. Armstrong, O.F.M. Cap., J.A. Wayne Hellmann, O.F.M. Conv., William J. Short, O.F.M. (New York: New City Press, 1999), 124.
3. *Powers of Horror, An Essay on Abjection,* trans., Leon S. Roudiez (New York: Columbia University Press, 1982), 127.

crucified." It is also from "within" that she understood not only the sufferings of Christ's body but those of his soul as well. More and more, she affirms that what happened to Christ on the cross no longer saddens her, but rather fills her with an indescribable joy. Witnessing a re-enactment of the Passion on the public square in Foligno, she says, "at the moment when it seemed to me one should weep… I was miraculously drawn into a state of such delight that I lost the power of speech and felt flat on the ground." At yet another moment recorded in the fifth supplementary step, in a vision that lasted three days, Christ and the Blessed Virgin appeared to her in their glorified state. In this same step, in a vision on Holy Saturday, Angela entered into the mystery of the Sacred Triduum. Rapt in a rare fusion of the erotic with the mystical, she sees herself with Christ in the sepulcher, kissing his breast then his mouth, from which a delightful fragrance emanated, then placing her cheek on Christ's own. He in turn, placing his hand on her other cheek, pressed her closely to him. Angela, having been married, knew well the gestures of human loving. In this intimate moment in the sepulcher with Christ, Angela experienced its infinite dimensions, physical expression transformed into the spiritual without the physical being denied.

Supplementary steps four and five contain further mystical experiences during the celebration of the Eucharist. On one particularly striking occasion, reminiscent of Francis' Canticle of Brother Sun but more feminine, God tells Angela that he will show her something of his power and "in an excess of wonder" over this manifestation she cries out: "This world is pregnant with God." On another, she relates that when she receives communion the host has a "most savory taste" and when it gradually descends into her body it makes her shake so violently that only with great effort can she then grasp the chalice.

Her visions in these five supplementary steps related to the Eucharist and to Christ crucified are impressive and central, but the formless visions from this period are even more striking. They suggest the mystical heights to which Angela had been elevated. In them Angela saw God through the attributes of some of his divine perfections such as beauty, wisdom, power, humility, justice, and often as the All Good. Although not as graphic as the earlier experiences, these contain far more suggestive and enticing power. The ineffable bursts alive in her, combining the transcendental and the personal, a state both sublime and totally inexpressible.

It is important to note that Angela's journey was shaped not only by her revelations and experiences of divine love, but also by periods of doubt and aridity, and strong diabolical temptations. Her experience reveals "the game of love" that God plays with a soul, a dialectics of presence and absence, even if for Angela each new ecstatic experience far exceeds whatever preceded it.

At the end of the fifth supplementary step Angela is so certain of God's love for her that she testifies to it to her scribe, Bro. A., through a series of examples. In the most striking one, she describes what happens when a soul has given hospitality to the Pilgrim. Since Bro. A resists her on this point, as he often did during his meetings with her, Angela replies: "Would that when you go to preach you could understand, as I understood when I had given hospitality to the Pilgrim. For then you would be absolutely unable to say anything about God, his infinite goodness being so far beyond anything you could possible say or think"... for "if you had attained this state, you would then say to people with total self-assurance: 'Go with God, because about God I can say nothing.' "

As she affirms again and again her certitude of the presence of God, Angela so unites herself and identifies with the love (a "pure love") and the will of Christ ("from two there was made one"), is so sure of herself and her judgments that she can declare having attained at once a complete knowledge of herself — her failings, poverty and unworthiness — and a true knowledge of the supereminent love of God, both together "in a totally indescribable way." Suddenly and inexplicably, however, this spiritual edifice collapses. And what takes place in the two final supplementary steps of the *Memorial* elevates Angela to the ranks of the greatest mystics within the Christian tradition. They contain some of the highest and most daring statements of mystical union ever expressed.

Nonetheless, Angela's experience during these two final steps, which took place over the course of a two-year period, disconcerts us. According to Bro. A., the most sublime visions and assurances of the presence of God were interlaced simultaneously with the greatest suffering and despair, the latter fading but not disappearing totally. How such opposite forms of consciousness could co-exist is difficult to understand.

Instruction IV, however, offers a possible hermeneutic for what happens in these final stages of the *Memorial*. An anonymous disciple reported, possibly four years after it had happened, that during an "illumination" while the Eucharist was being celebrated Angela was drawn and absorbed into the "fathomless abysses of God." Under the impact of this vision, the crucified God and man appeared to her and bestowed upon her soul, in a perfect manner," the double state of his own life": the total absorption in the experience of the sweetness of the uncreated God and the cruel death pangs of his crucifixion. Commenting further on the nature of the simultaneous reproduction of this double state, the scribe says that while in this illumination Angela was at once "filled with joy and sorrow ... sated with myrrh and honey, quasi-deified and crucified."

We can surmise then — even if it does not refer to the final steps of the Memorial — that the nature of the experience related in this Instruction resembles Angela's plunge into the agony and identification with Christ crucified, "the horrible darkness" of the sixth step and her immersion into the fathomless abysses of the Trinitarian life of the seventh step of the *Memorial*. The theological implications of such an experience have not yet been fully developed. In the Christian mystical tradition, only one experience comes close to Angela's, but does not contain its existential and torturous exemplification — John of the Cross' description of the blessings and the luminosity inherent in the dark night of the soul and of the spirit.

In these two final steps Angela seems to be sharing at an unprecedented level and depth the kenotic movement in which Christ manifests divine love completely. On the cross, he reaches the apex of the incarnational process when he empties himself of his divinity and, as in another context Angela herself asserts strikingly, becomes "poor of himself." By this very emptying and becoming poor Christ receives in one and the same movement the fullness and the riches of the divine life. This "illumination" reveals Angela's sharing in, her "inabyssation" or "transubstantiation" in the double state of Christ's life, at once "crucified and deified...."

Ultimately, however, how the two contrary experiences were mingled or to what extent they succeeded one another cannot be explained. For the sake of clarity one must follow Bro. A.'s lead and summarize them separately.

The Sixth Supplementary Step

The sixth step, then, is Angela's version of what John of the Cross later described more completely as the dark night of the soul. The storm "the horrible darkness," bearing down on Christ's faithful one devastated her body, but affected her soul even more deeply. The only comparison she could find to describe her soul's state was "that of a man hanged by the neck who with his hands tied behind him and his eyes blindfolded, remains dangling on the gallows and yet lives, with no help, no support, no remedy, swinging in the empty air." In this encounter with total despair, her body and soul trembling in uncontrollable agony, from the lowest depths there rose to Angela's consciousness the cry of final abandonment. Only the words of Christ on the cross, taking on, significantly, a mother's point of view, could articulate her anguish. Angela wailed and cried out repeatedly: "My son, my son, do not abandon me, my son!" The power and dialectic of Christ's burning love for her — a process of dying and rising, presence and absence — allowed Angela to enter his final agony and abandonment on the cross. Once again, a deep participation in the test of Christ's final hour illustrates most powerfully Angela's experience of profound abyss and dereliction, allowing us to grasp the meaning of her experience. In part, it shows how she identified with and participated in Christ's passion, approximating distantly the inaccessible mystery of the cross. Nevertheless, in her maternal paraphrase of Christ's last words, Angela identifies with them and articulates them in terms unique in the history of mystical literature.

In this step, Angela is immersed in a dark fire of purification meant to purge the very roots of self-love, unruly passions, resistance to God's will, and false self. Demons afflict her horribly. They not only remove the support of her virtues and revive familiar vices in her, but with uncontrollable fury also arouse and bring to the surface others she had never known before. Her body, she reports, is on fire — the residues of sexual disorder — and until forbidden from doing so, she actually cauterizes herself with burning coals. Angela also becomes aware, with dreadful lucidity, of her own sinfulness. She perceives herself as "house of the devil, a worker for and a dupe of demons, their daughter even devoid of all rectitude and virtue, and worthy of only the lowest part in hell." She even cries out for death, and beseeches God to send her to hell: "Since you have abandoned me," she howls, "make an end to it now and completely submerge me." She feels so very low as to have shared the lot of the damned in hell. Finally, the last vestige of her pride must be rooted out before she might find rest in the truth of her soul's relationship with God. Pure love demands that every illusion and every trace of self-satisfaction in any good accomplished be wiped away. Little wonder that, as the last remnants of resistance and rebellion rise from their hidden and unconscious sources to the surface, Angela's soul, in a state of havoc, rages against the night and her body swells in violent upheaval. Her torrent of words matches the torrent of experiences that assail her. No one can help nor can anyone console her, not even God himself. The torture is excruciating, "a veritable martyrdom," she asserts.

Angela needed to experience the crumbling of her most secure foundation in the divine life and dwell in the "horrible darkness" of this sixth step in order to be drawn into the depths and dazzling darkness of the Trinitarian life as described in the next and final step. This "extreme purification, humiliation and abasement," as she puts it at the end of this step, prepared her for a greater elevation in the seventh supplementary step, "the most wonderful of all."

The Seventh Supplementary Step

In the initial vision of this final step the light, the beauty and the fullness of God so dazzles Angela's ordinary senses that she is opened to a totally new experience of God.

Angela says that in this state, "I did not see love there. I then lost the love which was mine and was made nonlove," that is to say, a quality of loving that transcended what was described in previous steps concerning the nature of God's love for her or her own capacity to love him. Angela's love was transformed and invested, so to speak, with God's own ineffable mode of loving — some of the Instructions refer to an "uncreated love" — a love of pure relationality, one that abolishes the distinction between the lover and the beloved and perhaps even the loving in order to be pure love: an unmediated union with God

To further describe the initial stages of her union with God in this seventh supplementary step, Angela refers to divine darkness, an image drawn from the revival and development of apophatic mysticism during the century prior to Angela's birth. Medieval mystics commonly drew upon the writings of the Pseudo-Dyonisius and new translations and commentaries on his work to describe God's unknowability. Imparting to such Dyonisian apophatic language a subtlety uniquely hers, Angela asserts that "in" and "with" darkness she saw God as the "All Good" or the "secret Good." "In darkness" indicates the dimension of subjective blindness and "with darkness" suggests the transcendental obscurity of the Trinitarian life which she claims she is now perceiving. Angela further asserts that these dark visions contain degrees of elevation or attraction. In the highest modality, to which she says she was elevated three times, she found herself "standing or lying in the midst of the Trinity." More than anything else, the gravitational pull from the depths of God's Trinitarian life draws her: "When I am in that darkness I do not remember anything about anything human, or the God-man, or anything which has a form." Apparently, according to her perception, the most ineffable darkness, symbol of the depths of the Trinity, shades off into lesser intensity: the vision of the God-man. In this lesser darkness Angela beholds the eyes and the face of the God-man as he graciously and gently leans over to embrace her. While doing so he tells her, "You are I and I am you. " It is the celebrated moment of mystical marriage. Furthermore, in this lesser experience the vision of the God — man, which she says is hers continually, Angela claims such complete union and identity with him that the distinction between object and subject disappears. She even makes the daring claim that she was assured that there was "no longer any intermediary between God and herself." This bold and highly suspect contention resembles claims made by other medieval mystics, such as the Beguines Hadwijch, Mechtilde of Magdebourg and Marguerite Porete, as well as Jacopone da Todi, Eckhart, and Ruusbroec. They too, each with unique nuances, describe the summit of their mystical experience as consubstantial, without intermediary or distinction. In this mystical marriage "in" and "with" darkness described in the seventh step, Angela seems to be participating in the very movement in which the Son of God reveals the Father, the inaccessible and unrepresentable dimensions of the Trinity. In this secret good in which Angela claims to be enraptured, she further affirms that she sees "nothing that can be imagined or conceived" yet at the same time "knows everything she wants to know and possesses everything she wants to possess." Angela sees nothing and everything at once.

During this period of grace and plenitude Angela is blessed with visions that multiply like a kaleidoscope, ever changing and ever new, often blending into one another. "She swims," to use one of her expressions, in the boundless life of the Trinity, delighting in God's wisdom and judgments.

The dark visions that transmit a heightened awareness of God's transcendence were not, however, Angela's final revelation in this final step of the *Memorial.* There is much more. In a subsequent vision, she said that an "abyssal " attraction drew her ever more deeply into the Trinity with "unction and delights totally beyond any she had ever experienced." In this fathomless abyss, all previous supports — the life and humanity of Christ; the cross as bed to rest on; the considerations of the contempt, suffering and poverty experienced by the Son of God (to which she had just alluded in the sixth step); the visions of God in and with darkness — indeed, everything that could be named become nothing and fade in the background. Angela's uses relentless negation in her attempt to describe experiences that cannot be named.

In her final and supreme experiences, Angela distinguishes two modalities through which she experiences God in the innermost recesses of her soul. In the first, she perceives God manifested in "every creature and in everything that has being, in a devil and a good angel, in heaven and hell in good deeds and in adultery or homicide, in all things finally, which exist or have some degree of being whether beautiful or ugly." This modality, which seems to be a non-dual awareness of God, is continual. Furthermore, Angela affirms that in this state her soul is given a divine grace "that it cannot commit any offense."

In the second modality, God is manifest even more directly and the delights exceed, she says, "all that can be said or imagined." In this type of presence, during intermittent and diverse periods, Angela received the gift of penetrating the hidden meaning of the Holy Scriptures, "how some are saved and others are damned through them." Moreover in this region of the soul, where she sees that the All Good exists, there is a chamber, a place of stillness and rest "wherein no joy nor sadness can penetrate." Various other mystics have described the deepest and most inward part of the soul where God dwells. Eckhart calls it the "ground" or the "little castle"; Teresa of Avila, the "sparkling diamond"; John of the Cross, "the deepest center of the soul." In this state, Angela can also behold "the One who is and how he is the being of all creatures," the supreme mode of essence mysticism. Ultimately, "alone, purified and totally celestial," Angela hears God declaring that in her rests the entire Trinity: "You hold me and I hold you." From this place within the Trinity, "Christ's faithful one" understands "the complete truth that is in heaven and in hell, in the entire world, in every place, in all things, in every creature." The entire created universe becomes transparent, a knowledge by communion of the primal harmony of all that is, as seen from within its transcendent source. No part of creation is now strange or alienated. Everything finds its rightful place, its "complete truth."

Soaring from peak to peak in the highest reaches of the human spirit, Angela gives one last example of divine manifestation, one, as she asserts with each new revelation, greater and fuller than she had ever before experienced. On the feast of the Purification of Mary, she relates that she was granted to experience her own presentation within the immensity of the divine life. Immersed in these ineffable operations, ... "an operation of silence," Angela says that "the soul cannot understand itself, for it is no longer on earth but in heaven." In this state Angela also hears "most high words which cannot be repeated" and the assurance that henceforth "nothing can separate her from God." She even makes another bold and transgressive comparison, asserting that this state is "so deep and ineffable an abyss" that this form of presence to God is the "good which the saints enjoy in eternal life."

Throughout this last step of the *Memorial* Angela cries out repeatedly that "words crumble and fall," they "blaspheme," for ultimately, "nothing can explain God."

Perceiving that Angela, who some call "the queen of the explorers of the beyond," had attained such heights of mystical experience, Bro. A. decides to end the narration of the *Memorial* here. God assures both of them of the trustworthiness of everything that they had written by asserting that he "put his seal to it."

Angela 's life, nonetheless, does not end with the *Memorial.* Although she lived another thirteen years, the evolution of her mystical experiences was for the most part not documented. "My secret is mine," she kept repeating to those who solicited more revelations about her inner life. The second part of her

Book, the *Instructions*, reveals her role as a spiritual mother, "a teacher of theologians," as she has been called. Though very little is known about it, a small community gathered around Angela to listen to her teachings. She addressed a series of letters, reflections, and exhortations to disciples and admirers far and near, most notably the turbulent leader of the Spiritual Franciscans, Ubertino of Casale, who credited his conversion to her. Many of these instructions develop more fully themes alluded to in the *Memorial*, such as following Christ the suffering God-man in poverty, suffering and contempt, prayer, the Eucharist, knowledge of God and self, and the blessed Francis as model of prayer and poverty.

Notwithstanding Angela's reticence to say more about her personal life, the *Instructions* do record descriptions of some mystical experiences from the latter part of her life. The stunning *Instruction* XXIII recounts that, while meditating on the passion of Christ during Holy Week and trying to empty her soul of everything else, Angela heard this divine word sounding in her soul: "My love for you has not been a hoax." "These words," she said, "struck me a mortal blow. For immediately the eyes of my soul were opened and I saw that what he had said was true. I saw his acts of love, everything that the Son of God had done, all that he had endured in life and in death — this suffering God-man" and that "he had loved me with a most perfect and visceral love." On the other hand, "I saw the exact opposite in myself, because my love for him had never been anything but playing games, never true. Being made aware of this was a mortal blow and caused such intolerable pain that I thought I would die."

Finally, assembled in one discourse, are fragments of what Angela told her disciples during her final sickness (from a few days before Christmas, 1308, until 3 January 1309, the vigil of her death). Angela's last recorded words constitute a type of spiritual testament. In one final heart rending cry she exclaims:

"O unknown nothingness! O unknown nothingness! Truly, a soul cannot have a better awareness in this world than to perceive its own nothingness and to stay in its own cell."

Angela had been led into the abysses of the passionate and visceral love of the "suffering God-man" as expressed in his passion and death on the cross. Pushed to the limits of the possible and impossible, she felt more and more intensely the need to become empty, poor of every form of possession, to annihilate every image and representation, every word "for words blaspheme." In her journey into the obscure and yet dazzling darkness of God, she felt drawn from within to go beyond the duality of heaven and earth, good and evil, body and soul, and the divinity and the humanity of God to enter finally the space which is not a space, where the nothingness and the unknown abyss of self rejoin the unknown and ineffable nothingness of the divine life in the Trinity — a voluptuosity of suffering transformed into an infinite *jouissance.* Angela of Foligno, the passionate mystic of the double abyss and the queen of the explorers of the beyond.

Angela's Legacy

"I will do great things in you in the sight of the nations. Through you, I shall be known and my name will be praised by many nations." This annunciation at the beginning of the second supplementary step proved prophetic. Down through the ages, Angela's passionate and excessive love story and her spirituality have merited the esteem of an impressive number of saints, spiritual writers, and theologians and have inspired many others. It is not easy, however, to follow the stream of her influence. Following are some of the more salient moments in which her direct influence on subsequent spiritual literature has sprung up and watered souls thirsty for the absolute.

The most resent research on the early fortunes of Angela's *Book* stress its political nature, its involvement with and transmission by the Spiritual Franciscans, who, likely, made Angela into one of their champions. Because they resisted the accommodations of Francis' primitive ideal by mainstream Franciscans, the Spirituals were persecuted and some even burned at the stake. It is likely that by association, Angela's *Book* suffered a similar fate and had to go underground; thus one of the trademarks of her *Book* — its anonymity. Her name is not mentioned nor is that of her scribe, her companion, or the lectors and holy men who read her *Book* and gave it their seal of approval. Nor that of Foligno, where the work has its main setting. Aside from a brief reference by Ubertino of Casale, one of the persecuted leaders of the Spirituals, no early chronicles of the Order mention Angela. Only after nearly a century of almost absolute silence concerning her does Angela begin to appear, especially among the Observants, a reform wing of the Franciscan family. The interest in Angela's writings among this new branch of Franciscans climaxes with the first positively known printings of Angela's *Book*, promoted by the Spanish cardinal Francesco Ximenes, an Observant: a Spanish version in 1510, and a Latin version in 1555. This is the edition of her writings that likely made its way to the hands of Teresa of Avila (d.1582), who uses Angela's language to describe the trials of the sixth mansion in her *Interior Castle.* The oft-quoted verse of one of Teresa's poems, "I die because I do not die," can be found in the seventh supplementary step of Angela's *Memorial.* It is also interesting to note that in 1519 five copies of Angela's book were part of the library that a group of Spanish Franciscans carried on their way to evangelize the New World.

In the seventeenth century, others who were influenced by and refer to Angela include Francis de Sales, Alphonsus Liguori, Pope Benedict XIV, Fenelon, Bossuet, and Jean Jacques Olier. In the late nineteenth century, a brilliant if faulty translation by the French philosopher Ernest Hello — *Le livre des visions et instructions de la bienheureuse Angèle de Foligno* — catapulted Angela's Book (75,000 copies, ten editions) into the consciousness of contemporary French culture. The writings of novelist George Bernanos, the poet-philosopher George Bataille, the visionary theologian Teilhard de Chardin, as well as prominent French feminists such as Simone de Beauvoir, Julia Kristeva, and Luce Irigaray quote Angela. Another example that reveals the influence of Hello's version is a play adapted from it by Philipe Clévenot, starring Bérangère Bonvoisin as Angela. *Celle qui ment* is the title of the play performed in Paris and Rouen in 1984. More recently the Italian director Enrico Bellani produced a film on Angela's life, *La mistica Angela*; noteworthy also is an award winning theatrical and musical production by Rosaria La Russo and Roberta Vacca, *Spirito versus Natura*. Aside from the publication of a series of international congresses held in Foligno and annual sessions dedicated to her at the International Congress on Medieval Studies (Western Michigan University, Kalamazoo, Michigan) the more notable new scholarly works on Angela include, *Angèle de Foligno, Le Dossier*, edited by Giulia Barone and Jacques Dalarun (Rome: Ecole Francaise de Rome, 1999). Giovanni Pozzi, *Il libro dell'esperienza* (Milan: Adelphi edizioni, 2001). An international bibliography, being prepared by Sergio Andreoli, Paul Lachance, and Francesco Santi, will be available soon in book form and on a web site produced by the Ezio Franceschini foundation in Florence, Italy. In Foligno, the Conventual Franciscans sponsor the *Cenacolo della Beata Angela*, a center containing research material and providing a tour of the sites surrounding Angela's life.

Angela was beatified on 11 July 1701 and her feast day is celebrated on January 4. Although often referred to as a saint, Angela has never been canonized. A commission is currently working on this project.

Selections from the Memorial

Prologue

Those who are truly faithful know what it is to probe, perceive, and touch the Incarnate Word of Life as he himself affirms in the Gospel: "If anyone loves me, he will keep my word, and my Father will love him, and we shall come to him and make our dwelling place with him." And, "he who loves me, I will reveal myself to him."

God himself enables his faithful ones to fully verify this experience and the teaching about such an experience. Recently, he has once again revealed something of this experience and this teaching, through one of his faithful, to increase the devotion of his people. In the pages that follow, there is an incomplete, very weak and abridged, but nonetheless true description of it.

Selections from the First Twenty Steps

Awareness of Sinfulness

The first step is the awareness of one's sinfulness, in which the soul greatly fears being damned to hell. In it the soul weeps bitterly.

Confession of Sins

The second step is the confession of sins. The soul still experiences shame and bitterness. There is not yet the feeling of love, only grief. She also told me how she had often received communion in a state of sin because she had been too ashamed to make a full confession. Day and night her conscience reproached her. And, when she prayed to the blessed Francis to find her a confessor who knew sins well, someone she could fully confess herself to, that very same night an elderly friar appeared to her and told her: "Sister, if you had asked me sooner, I would have complied with your request sooner. Nonetheless, your request is granted."

The very next morning, I went to the church of Saint Francis but left it quickly. On my return home I entered the cathedral of Saint Felician where I saw a friar preaching, the chaplain of the bishop. Prompted by the Lord, I decided on the spot to confess myself to him....

Self-knowledge

The fifth step is the knowledge of self. Partially enlightened, the soul sees nothing but defects in itself, and condemns itself before God as most certainly worthy of hell. This is a source of much bitter weeping.

The Healing of Memories

The sixth step consists of a certain illumination through which my soul was graced with a deeper awareness of all my sins. In this illumination, I saw that I had offended all the creatures that had been made for me. In a very profound way, all my sins surged back into my memory, even as I confessed them before God. I asked all the creatures whom I felt I had offended not to accuse me. And then, I was given to pray with a great fire of love. I invoked all the saints, and the Blessed Virgin, to intercede for me and to pray to that love which previously had granted me such great favors, to make what was dead in me come to life. As a result, it did seem to me that all creatures had mercy on me, and all the saints.

Gazing at the Cross

In the seventh step I was given the grace of beginning to look at the cross on which I saw Christ who had died for us. What I saw was still without savor, but it did cause me much grief....

The Need to Strip Oneself

In the eighth step, while looking at the cross, I was given an even greater perception of the way the Son of God had died for our sins. This perception made me aware of all my sins, and this was extremely painful. I felt that I myself had crucified Christ. But I still did not know which was the greatest gift he had bestowed — whether it was the fact that he had withdrawn me from sin and hell and converted me to the way of penance or that he had been crucified for me. Nonetheless, this perception of the meaning of the cross set me so afire that, standing near the cross, I stripped myself of all my clothing and offered my whole self to him. Although very fearful, I promised him then to maintain perpetual chastity and not to offend him again with any of my bodily members, accusing each of these one by one. I prayed that he himself keep me faithful to this promise, namely, to observe chastity with all the members of my body and all my senses. On the one hand, I feared to make this promise, but on the other hand, the fire of which I spoke drew it out of me, and I could not do otherwise.

The Path of Thorns and Tribulations

In the ninth step, it was given to me to seek the way of the cross, that I too might stand at the foot of the cross where all sinners find refuge. I was instructed, illumined, and shown the way of the cross in the following manner: I was inspired with the thought that if I wanted to go to the cross, I would need to strip myself in order to be lighter and go naked to it. This would entail forgiving all who had offended me, stripping myself of everything worldly, of all attachments to men and women, of my friends and relatives, and everyone else, and, likewise, of my possessions and even my very self. Then I would be free to give my heart to Christ from whom I had received so many graces, and to walk along the thorny path, that is, the path of tribulations. I then decided to put aside my best garments, fine food, and fancy head-dress. But this was still a very shameful and burdensome thing for me to do, for at this point I was not feeling any love. During this period I was still living with my husband, and it was bitter for me to put up with all the slanders and injustices. Nonetheless, I bore these as patiently as I could. Moreover, it came to pass, God so willing, that at that time my mother, who had been a great obstacle to me, died. In like manner my husband died, as did all my sons in a short space of time. Because I had already entered the aforesaid way, and had prayed to God for their death, I felt a great consolation when it happened. I thought that since God had conceded me this aforesaid favor, my heart would always be within God's heart, and God's heart always within mine.

Christ Shows His Wounds to Angela

In the tenth step, while I was asking God what I could do to please him more, in his mercy, he appeared to me many times, both while I was asleep and awake, crucified on the cross. He told me that I should look at his wounds. In a wonderful manner, he showed me how he had endured all these wounds for me; and he did this many times. As he was showing me the sufferings he had endured for me from each of these wounds, one after the other, he told me: "What then can you do that would seem to you to be enough?" Likewise, he appeared many times to me while I was awake, and these appearances were more pleasant than those which occurred while I was asleep, although he always seemed to be suffering greatly. He spoke to me just as he had while I was sleeping, showing me his afflictions from head to toe. He even showed me how his beard, eyebrows, and hair had been plucked out and enumerated each and every one of the blows of the whip that he had received. And he said, "I have endured all these things for you."

Resolution to Become Poor

In the twelfth step, as it did not seem to me that there was any penance harsh enough to meet my need to break away from the world, I resolved then and there to give up absolutely everything and really do the kind of penance I felt called to do and come to the cross as God had inspired me. The grace to make this resolution was given to me by God in the following wonderful manner. I ardently desired to become poor, and I was often greatly disturbed by the thought that death could very well surprise me before I could do so. But I was also assailed by numerous contrary temptations. I imagined, for instance, that because of my youth, begging could be dangerous and shameful for me; that I might die of hunger, cold, and nakedness. Moreover, everyone tried to dissuade me from my resolution to become poor. At that moment, however, through the mercy of God, a great light came into my heart and with it, a firm resolve which I believed then, and still believe, will last for eternity. In that light, I made up my mind and decided that even if I had to die of hunger, shame, or nakedness, as long as this pleased God or could please God, I would in no way give up my resolve on account of those things. Even if I were certain all those evils would befall me, I know I would die happy in God. From then on my mind was made up.

Cleansed by the Blood of Christ

In the fourteenth step, while I was standing in prayer, Christ on the cross appeared more clearly to me while I was awake, that is to say, he gave me an even greater awareness of himself than before. He then called me to place my mouth to the wound in his side. It seemed to me that I saw and drank the blood which was freshly flowing from his side. His intention was to make me understand that by this blood he would cleanse me. And at this I began to experience a great joy, although when I thought about the passion I was still filled with sadness.

"How Sluggish the Soul's Progress!"

[...] At each of these previous steps, I lingered for a good while before I was able to move on to the next step. In some of the steps I lingered longer, and not so long in others. At which point, Christ's faithful one also expressed her amazement: "Oh! Nothing is written here about how sluggish the soul's progress is! How bound it is, how shackled are its feet, and how ill-served it is by the world and the devil."

Entry into Mystical Consciousness

Afterwards, in the seventeenth step, it was shown to me that the Blessed Virgin had obtained for me the grace of a faith different from the one I had before. For it seemed to me as if, in contrast to what I now experienced, my former faith had been lifeless and my tears forced.

[...] Among her many dreams and visions, she related the following. Once I was in the cell where I had enclosed myself for the Great Lent. I was enjoying and meditating on a certain saying in the Gospel, a saying which I found of great value and extremely delightful. I had by my side a book, a missal, and I thirsted to see that saying again in writing. With great difficulty I contained myself and resisted opening this book in my hands, for I feared I might do so out of pride or out of too great a thirst and love. I became drowsy and fell asleep still in the throes of this desire. Immediately, I was led into a vision, and I was told that the understanding of the Epistle is something so delightful that if one grasped it properly one would completely forget everything belonging to this world. And he who was leading me asked me: "Do you want to have this experience?" As I agreed and ardently desired it, he immediately led me into this experience. From it I understood how sweet it is to experience the riches of God and I immediately and completely forgot the world. He who was leading me added that the understanding of the Gospel is even more delightful, so much more so that if one understood it one would not only forget the world but even oneself, totally. He led me still further and enabled me to directly experience this. Immediately I understood what it is to experience the riches of God and derived such delight from it that I not only forgot the world but even myself. This state was so delightful and holy that I begged the one who was leading me not to let me ever leave it. He replied that what I was asking was still not possible; and he immediately led me back to myself. I opened my eyes and felt an immense joy from what I had seen but also great sorrow at having lost it. Recalling this experience still gives me great pleasure. From then on, I was filled with such certitude, such light, and such ardent love of God that I went on to affirm, with the utmost certainty, that nothing of these delights of God is being preached. Preachers cannot preach it; they do not understand what they preach. He who was leading me into this vision told me so.

The Fire of the Love of God

[...] Afterwards, this fire of the love of God in my heart became so intense that if I heard anyone speak about God I would scream. Even if someone had stood over me with an axe ready to kill me, this would not have stopped my screaming. This happened to me for the first time when I sold my country villa to give to the poor. It was the best property that I owned.[...] Also, whenever I saw the passion of Christ depicted, I could hardly bear it, and I would come down with a fever and fall sick. My companion, as a result, hid paintings of the passion or did her best to keep them out of my sight.

The Promise of the Indwelling of the Trinity

[...] On another occasion, before she had completely finished distributing all her belongings, she told me that one evening, while she was at prayer, it seemed to her that she felt nothing of God and so she prayed and lamented in these terms: "Lord, whatever I am doing, I do only to find you. Will I find you after I've finished what I have undertaken?" And she asked for many other things in that prayer. The response was: "What do you want?" To this she replied: "I want neither gold nor silver; even if you should offer me the whole universe, I would not be satisfied. I want only you." And then he answered: "Hurry, for as soon as you have finished what you have set out to do the whole Trinity will come into you."

First Supplementary Step

The Pilgrimage to Assisi

[Christ's faithful one] started by saying that during her trip to Assisi (about which I was questioning her), she was in a state of prayer all along the way. And among other things, she had asked blessed Francis to ask God on her behalf that she might feel Christ's presence; and likewise to obtain from him the grace of observing well the rule of blessed Francis which she had recently promised; and above all for this: that he would make her become, and end up, truly poor.

[...] as soon as I had genuflected at the entrance of the church and when I saw a stained glass window depicting Saint Francis being closely held by Christ, I heard him telling me: "Thus I will hold you closely to me and much more closely than can be observed with the eyes of the body. And now the time has come, sweet daughter, my temple, my delight, to fulfill my promise to you. I am about to leave you in the form of this consolation, but I will never leave you if you love me."

Bitter in some ways as these words were for me to hear, I nonetheless experienced them above all as sweet, the sweetest I have ever heard. Then I turned my gaze on the one speaking to me so that I might also see him not only with the eyes of the body but also with those of the spirit. I, brother, interrupted at this point to ask her: "What did you see?" She replied: "I saw something full of such immense majesty that I do not know how to describe it, but it seemed to me that it was the All Good. Moreover, he spoke many words of endearment as he withdrew from me. And he withdrew, ah! so very gently and so very gradually.

"Love Still Unknown, Why Do You Leave Me?"

After he had withdrawn, I began to shout and to cry out without any shame: "Love still unknown, why do you leave me?" I could not nor did I scream out any other words than these: "Love still unknown, why? why? why?" Furthermore, these screams were so choked up in my throat that the words were unintelligible. Nonetheless what remained with me was a certitude that God, without any doubt, had been speaking to me. As I shouted I wanted to die. It was very painful for me not to die and to go on living. After this experience I felt my bones become dislocated.

An Inexpressible Sweetness

[...]Once I was back home, I felt so peaceful and was so filled with divine sweetness that I find no words to express my experience; and there was also in me a desire to die. The thought that I had to go on living was a great burden because of that inexpressible sweetness, quiet, peace, and delight which I felt; and because I wanted to attain the source of this experience and not lose it — that is why I wanted to leave this world. The thought of continuing to live was a greater burden for me to bear than the pain and sorrow I had felt over the death of my mother and my sons, and beyond any pain that I could imagine. I lay at home enthralled by this great consolation and in a state of languor for eight days. And my soul cried out: "Lord, take pity on me and do not allow me to remain any longer in this world." On the road going to Assisi, he had predicted that I would experience this delectable and indescribable consolation in these terms: "Once back in your home, you will feel a sweetness different from any you have ever experienced. And I will not speak to you then as I have until now; but you will feel me." True enough I did feel this sweet and ineffable consolation in which I felt so peaceful and quiet that I cannot find words to describe it. I lay in bed for eight days hardly able to speak, say the Our Father, or get up to move around. He had also told me on the road to Assisi: "I was with the apostles many times, and they saw me with their bodily eyes but they did not feel what you feel. You do not see me but you feel me."

"The Ring of God's Love"

I realized at this point that this experience was coming to an end, for he began to withdraw from me and he did so very gently while telling me: "My daughter, you are sweeter to me than I am to you." And he repeated what he had already said: "My temple, my delight." At these words, I realized that he didn't want me to be lying down while he was leaving so I stood up. He then said to me: "You are holding the ring of my love. From now on you are engaged to me and you will never leave me. May the blessing of the Father, the Son, and the Holy Spirit be upon you and your companion." He said this at the moment of departure because I had asked him for a special grace for my companion. In response to this request he simply said: "The grace I will give to your companion will be a different one than yours." I must add that when he said: "You shall never leave me again," my soul cried out: "Oh, that I may never sin mortally." To this he replied: "These are your words, not mine."

Extraordinary Fragrances

Thereafter, I often smelled scents of extraordinary fragrances. But these experiences and others were so powerful that I cannot find words to describe them. I can say something about them, but my words are inadequate to transmit the sweetness and the delight I experienced. Many more times did I hear God speak to me with words such as the above but never at such length, nor with the same depth or with such sweetness.

Angela's Aura

[...] Later, [Angela's] companion told me, brother scribe, that on one occasion when Christ's faithful one was lying on her side in a state of ecstasy, she saw something like a splendid, magnificent star shining with a wonderful and countless variety of colors. Rays of astonishing beauty, some thick, others slender, radiated from Christ's faithful one. Emanating from her breast while she was lying on her side, the rays unfolded or coiled as they ascended upwards towards heaven. She saw this with her bodily eyes while she was wide awake, near the third hour. The star was not very big.

The Trinity Enters Angela's Soul

[...] Since I still doubted that the Father, Son, and Holy Spirit had entered into me, unworthy as I am, and imagined that perhaps this had been said to deceive me, it was then repeated to me several times: "It is indeed the Trinity that has entered into you. Ask Brother A. again how this could be possible." Then I was also told that in this exchange the Father, Son, and Holy Spirit were speaking to me; and that, or so it seemed to me, I was being told that the Trinity was at once one, and a union of many. Then, as a further explanation, the example of the sun as well as other examples were presented to me, but I rejected these, for when I hear such great things I push them aside fearfully because I feel unworthy of them. What I wanted was that God would make me actually feel that on this point, the presence of the Holy Trinity in me, I could not be deceived.

The Beauty of Christ

[...] This is what she said to me: Once when I was meditating on the great suffering which Christ endured on the cross, I was considering the nails which, I had heard it said, had driven a little bit of the flesh of his hands and feet into the wood. And I desired to see at least that small amount of Christ's flesh which the nails had driven into the wood. And then such was my sorrow over the pain that Christ had endured that I could no longer stand on my feet. I bent over and sat down; I stretched out my arms on the ground and inclined my head on them. Then Christ showed me his throat and his arms.

And then my former sorrow was transformed into a joy so intense that I can say nothing about it. This was a new joy, different from the others. I was so totally absorbed by this vision that I wasn't able to see, hear, or feel anything else. My soul saw this vision so clearly that I have no doubts about it, nor will I ever question it. I was so certain of the joy which remained in my soul that henceforth I don't believe I will ever lose this sign of God's presence. Such also was the beauty of Christ's throat or neck that I concluded that it must be divine. Through this beauty it seemed to me that I was seeing Christ's divinity, and that I was standing in the presence of God; but of that moment that is all I remember seeing. I do not know how to compare the clarity and brightness of that vision with anything or any color in the world except, perhaps, the clarity and brightness of Christ's body which I sometimes see at the elevation of the host.

Eucharistic Visions

When I, the brother who is writing this, heard what I believe God had wanted her to say concerning the vision of the body of Christ, I immediately noted it in my heart. Then I questioned and compelled her to tell me everything she had ever seen in this vision of the body of Christ. Under pressure from me, she began to talk: Sometimes I see the host itself just as I saw that neck or throat, and it shines with such splendor and beauty that it seems to me that it must come from God; it surpasses the splendor of the sun. This beauty which I see makes me conclude with the utmost certainty and without a shadow of a doubt that I am seeing God. When I was at home, however, the vision of Christ's neck or throat which I saw was even more beautiful, so beautiful that I believe I will never lose the joy of it. I have no way to compare it except with the vision of the host containing the body of Christ, for in the host I see a beauty which far surpasses the beauty of the sun. My soul is in great distress because I am truly unable to describe this vision.

She also told me that sometimes she sees the host in a different way, that is, she sees in it two most splendid eyes, and these are so large that it seems only the edges of the host remain visible. Once even, not in the host but in the monstrance, I saw the eyes and these were of such beauty and so delightful to look at that, as with the vision of the neck, I don't believe I will ever lose the joy of that vision. Though I do not know if I was asleep or awake I found myself once again in a state of great and ineffable joy, one so great that I do not believe I could ever lose it.

On another occasion she said she had seen the Christ Child in the host. He appeared to her as someone tall and very lordly, as one holding dominion. He also seemed to hold something in his hand as a sign of his dominion, and he sat on a throne. But I cannot say what he was holding in his hands. I saw this with my bodily eyes, as I did everything I ever saw of the host. When this vision occurred I did not kneel down like the others and I can't recall whether I ran right up to the altar or whether I was unable to move because I was in such a delightful contemplative state. I know that I was also very upset because the priest put down the host on the altar too quickly. Christ was so beautiful and so magnificently adorned. He looked like a child of twelve. This vision was a source of such joy for me that I don't believe I will ever lose the joy of it. I was also so sure of it that I do not doubt a single detail of it. Hence it is not necessary for you to write it. I was even so delighted by that vision that I did not ask him to help me nor did I have anything good or bad to say. I simply delighted in seeing that inestimable beauty.

Second Supplementary Step

God's Exclusive Love for Angela

[...] During this same period, while I was once again in prayer, I suddenly heard him speaking to me very graciously in these words: "My daughter, sweeter to me than I am to you, my temple, my delight, the heart of God almighty is now upon your heart." And these words were accompanied with a feeling of God's presence far greater than I had ever experienced. All the members of my body thrilled with delight as I lay in this experience.

He said: "God almighty has deposited much love in you, more than in any woman of this city. He takes delight in you and is fully satisfied with you and your companion. Try to see to it that your lives are a light for all those who wish to look upon them. A harsh judgment awaits those who look at your lives but do not act accordingly."

A Sign of God's Love

[...] Then he said to me: I am about to give you a much better sign than the one you asked for [a tangible sign]. This sign will be continuously in the depths of your soul and from it you will always feel something of God's presence and be burning with love for him. And you will recognize in your deep self that no one but I can do such a thing. Here then is the sign which I deposit in the depths of your soul, one better that the one you asked for: I deposit in you a love of me so great that your soul will be continually burning for me.

God "As a Fullness, a Brightness"

Christ's faithful one then told me that she saw God, and when I, brother scribe, asked her how or what she saw, and if she saw something with a bodily form, she responded as follows: I saw a fullness, a brightness with which I felt myself so filled that words fail me, nor can I find anything to compare it with. I cannot tell you that I saw something with a bodily form, but he was as he is in heaven, namely, of such an indescribable beauty that I do not know how to describe it to you except as the Beauty and the All Good. And all the saints were standing before the divine majesty and praising him. But as for myself, it seemed to me that I stood in that presence only a little while.

No One Can Be Excused for Not Being Saved

[...] Christ's faithful one spoke to me as follows: I have just recently been told the following, and it has been so impressed on my heart that I can scarcely hold myself back from crying it out and proclaiming it to all, so clearly has he manifested this truth to me: No one can find an excuse for not being saved, for nothing more is required than to do what a sick person does with his doctor, that is, to show one's infirmity to him and dispose oneself to do what he says. Thus one should do nothing more, nor rely on any other medicine for oneself, but just show oneself to the doctor and dispose oneself to do everything the doctor orders; and take care not to mix in anything contrary to what he prescribes. My soul then understood that the medicine was his blood and he himself was the one who administers this medicine to the sick. And this entails nothing more for the one who is sick than to have the proper disposition so that the doctor can restore one's health and heal one's infirmity.

The Fire of Sweet and Gentle Love

[...] I, brother scribe, interrupted at this point to ask her if in this experience (at the moment of elevation of the host) she saw something else in the body of Christ, something similar to what she was accustomed to seeing on other occasions. Her response was no, but she said that she truly felt Christ in her soul. To this, I, brother, pressed her further: "How do you know that this is truly so?" And she responded as follows: Because there is nothing that sets the soul ablaze as when Christ is in the soul and delights it with his love. For then it was not like the fire with which the soul is sometimes ablaze but was the fire of sweet and gentle love. For my part I do not doubt when such a fire is in the soul because the soul then knows that God is truly present for no other could produce this effect. When this happens all the members feel a disjointing, and I wish it to be so. Indeed such is the extreme delight that I feel that I would want to always remain in this state. Furthermore I hear the bones cracking when they are thus disjointed. I feel this disjointing more when the body of Christ is elevated. It is especially then that my hands suffer this disjointing and open.

Third Supplementary Step

Those Invited to a Special Table

[...] Then, with my soul very pleased by what it was hearing, I asked him: "Tell me, Lord, when do you send out this invitation to everyone?" And he answered: "I have called and invited everyone to eternal life. Those who wish to come, let them come; for no one can give the excuse of not being called. And if you want to understand how much I loved and wanted them at my table, simply look at the cross." Afterwards he added: "Behold, those called are coming, and being placed at the table." And he also made it understood that he himself was the table and the food which he was offering. I then asked: "By which way did those who were called come?" To this he replied: "By way of tribulation, such as happens to the virgins, the chaste, the poor, the long-suffering, and the sick." And he proceeded to name the many categories of those who are to be saved. I understood both his reasoning and his explanations, and every word I heard was a source of great delight. I even strove to keep my eyes perfectly still so as to stay with this consolation. The above-mentioned, therefore, are those who are commonly called "sons." What he was trying to get me to understand in telling me this was that virginity, poverty, fever, the loss of sons, tribulations, and the loss of possessions are all sent by God. He named all these and gave the motive and explanation for their occurrence, which I fully understood. And he said all these are sent by God to those who are called "sons" for their own good. But when these things happen, the sons do not understand why, nor do they ponder over their meaning, and they are even troubled by them at first. It is only afterwards when they come to the realization that these things are sent by God that they are able to endure them peacefully. The ones, however, who are invited to a special table, and those whom the Lord leads to eat from his own plate and drink from his own cup are those who wish to know who this good man is who invited them, so that they may learn how to please him. Once they become aware that they received this invitation without any merit or worth on their part, they then actively set out to please him. For they know then that they are much loved by God and are truly unworthy of this love. And because of this awareness, they go to the cross to fix their attention and regard upon it, and therein discover what love is.

Sweetness in the midst of Tribulations

[...] Since I, brother scribe, questioned her about the above, Christ's faithful one, in reply, sought to reaffirm how true it was that the sons of God feel divine sweetness in the midst of the persecutions and tribulations they suffer, as it was demonstrated to her in such a wonderful manner in the instruction from God just written. So she began to relate an example drawn from her own life, pointing out that when she had been persecuted by the friars and the "continents," she could find no words to express the quality of the sweetness she felt or the abundant tears of joy she experienced like an anointing. I likewise challenged what she had said to me concerning the aforesaid teachings she had received from God on the theme of the sons of God; how the special sons eat from the same plate and drink from the same cup as Christ; and how, even if they initially experience this eating and drinking as bitter, it nonetheless becomes sweet for them, and indeed most delectable — I insisted that their experience was a bitter one. In response, Christ's faithful one related a story to me through which she tried to show me that it was not bitter but sweet.

Finding Christ among the Lepers

This is what she told me: On Maundy Thursday, I suggested to my companion that we go out to find Christ: "Let's go," I told her, "to the hospital and perhaps we will be able to find Christ among the poor, the suffering, and the afflicted." We brought with us all the head veils that we could carry, for we had nothing else. We told Giliola, the servant at that hospital, to sell them and from the sale to buy some food for those in the hospital to eat. And, although initially she strongly resisted our request, and said we were trying to shame her into doing so, nonetheless, because of our repeated insistence, she went ahead and sold our small head veils and from the sale bought some fish. We had also brought with us all the bread which had been given to us to live on. And after we had distributed all that we had, we washed the feet of the women and the hands of the men, and especially those of one of the lepers which were festering and in an advanced stage of decomposition. Then we drank the very water with which we had washed him. And the drink was so sweet that, all the way home, we tasted its sweetness and it was as if we had received Holy Communion. As a small scale of the leper's sores was stuck in my throat, I tried to swallow it. My conscience wouldn't let me spit it out, just as if I had received Holy Communion. I really didn't want to spit it out but simply to detach it from my throat.

Fourth Supplementary Step

The World Is Pregnant with God

[...] Afterwards [God] added: "I want to show you something of my power." And immediately the eyes of my soul were opened, and in a vision I beheld the fullness of God's presence in which I beheld and comprehended the whole of creation, that is, what is on this side and what is beyond the sea, the abyss, the sea itself, and everything else. And in everything that I saw, I could perceive nothing except the presence of the power of God, and in a manner totally indescribable. And my soul in an excess of wonder cried out: "This world is pregnant with God!" Wherefore I understood how small is the whole of creation — that is, what is on this side and what is beyond the sea, the abyss, the sea itself, and everything else — but the power of God fills it all to overflowing.

The Game God Plays with the Soul

Christ's faithful one also told me, brother scribe: After I had heard the above, God often and repeatedly accomplished wonders for my soul which I understood no one could make possible save God alone. For example, once my soul was lifted up in God and my joy was so great that if it lasted I believe that my body would immediately lose the use of all its senses and all its members. God often plays like this with and in the soul. When the soul tries to seize him, he immediately withdraws. The soul nonetheless remains in a state of great joy, and this joy is accompanied by a certitude that it is God who is at work, and in no way can it doubt this in the least. I can provide no comparison nor give a name to what I see or feel in this experience. In the past this experience was usually different from what it is now, but at all times it is totally indescribable.

Christ Embracing the Soul

[...]Once I was at Vespers and was gazing at the cross. And while I was thus gazing at the cross with the eyes of the body, suddenly my soul was set ablaze with love; and every member of my body felt it with the greatest joy. I saw and felt that

Christ was within me, embracing my soul with the very arm with which he was crucified. This took place right at the moment when I was gazing at the cross or shortly afterwards. The joy that I experienced to be with him in this way and the sense of security that he gave me were far greater than I had ever been accustomed to.

Fifth Supplementary Step

The Poverty of Christ

Christ's faithful one related it as follows: Once I was meditating on the poverty of the Son of God incarnate. I saw his poverty — its greatness was demonstrated to my heart, to the extent that he wished me to see it — and I saw those for whom he had made himself poor. I then experienced such sorrow and remorse that I almost fainted. God wanted to demonstrate to me even more of his poverty. And I saw him poor of friends and relatives. I even saw him poor of himself and so poor that he seemed powerless to help himself. It is sometimes said that the divine power was then hidden out of humility. But even if this has been said, I say that God's power was not hidden then, because he himself has taught me otherwise. From this vision of the poverty of the Son of God, I experienced and felt an even greater sorrow than before, for in it I recognized so much of my own pride that joy was no longer possible.

The Immensity of Christ's Passion

Another time, I was once again standing in prayer and meditating sorrowfully on the passion of the Son of God incarnate. Then, through God's will, the passion was shown to me, that is, he himself granted me to see more of his passion than I have ever been told, and he saw that I perceived more of his passion than I have ever heard spoken of. For Christ had foreseen all the hearts impiously hardened against him, everyone contriving to destroy his name, and how they constantly kept in mind their purpose to destroy him. He had also foreseen all the subtle cunning they employed against him, the Son of God; their manifold designs and plans, and the extent of their rage against him; all their preparations and everything they thought about how they could even more cruelly afflict him — for the cruel sufferings of his passion were indeed acute and manifold. And he had also seen all the sufferings, the injuries, and the shame he would be submitted to. All this my soul was aware of, and it saw more of his passion than I want to tell; I don't want at this point to say anything more about it. Then my soul cried out loudly: "O holy Mary, mother of the afflicted one, tell me something of your Son's pain which no one else but you can possibly recall. For you saw more of his passion than any other saint; and as I perceive it, you not only saw it with your bodily eyes, but also pictured it with your imagination, and out of the continual ardent devotion that was yours toward the one you loved." At this point, my soul cried out in extreme pain: "Is there any saint who can tell me something of this passion which I have not yet heard spoken of or related, but which my soul has seen, which is so great that I find no words to express it?" My soul saw such suffering! At this point, Christ's faithful one, in an explanation of the above, told me, brother scribe, that her soul had seen so much of the passion that it understood that even though the Blessed Virgin had seen more of it and mentioned more of its details than any other saint, still she herself could not — and neither could any other saint — find words to express it. Christ's faithful one said she understood this so well that if any saint were to try to express it, she would tell him: "Are you the one who sustained it?" Christ's faithful one also added: My pain, then, exceeded by far any that I had ever experienced. That my body could not sustain me then should not be cause for wonder, for at that point I could feel no joy. I indeed lost my usual capacity for joy, and during this period it was impossible for me to recover it.

Two Wills Made One

[...] Likewise, divine goodness granted me, afterwards, the grace that from two there was made one, because I could not will anything except as he himself willed. How great is the mercy of the one who realized this union! — it almost completely stabilized my soul. I possessed God so fully that I was no longer in my previous customary state but was led to find a peace in which I was united with God and was content with everything.

The Kiss in the Sepulcher

[...] On Holy Saturday, after what has just been related, Christ's faithful one told me the wonderful and joy-filled experiences of God's presence which were now hers. Among other things, she related to me, brother scribe, that on that very day, in a state of ecstasy, she found herself in the sepulcher with Christ. She said she had first of all kissed Christ's breast — and saw that he lay dead, with his eyes closed — then she kissed his mouth, from which, she added, a delightful fragrance emanated, one impossible to describe. This moment lasted only a short while. Afterwards, she placed her cheek on Christ's own and he, in turn, placed his hand on her other cheek, pressing her closely to him. At that moment, Christ's faithful one heard him telling her: "Before I was laid in the sepulcher, I held you this tightly to me." Even though she understood that it was Christ telling her this, nonetheless she saw him lying there with eyes closed, lips motionless, exactly as he was when he lay dead in the sepulcher. Her joy was immense and indescribable.

God's Love Moving like a Sickle

Once, during this same Lent, as Christ's faithful one further told me, it seemed to her that she was in a state of great spiritual aridity. She prayed to God that he give her something of himself for she felt very dry and deprived of every good. And then the eyes of her soul were opened and she had a vision of love gently advancing toward her. She saw the beginning of it but not the end, only its continuation; and for the color of this love, she could find no comparison. And suddenly she saw it coming towards her with the eyes of her soul, more clearly than can be seen with the eyes of the body, and as it approached her it moved like a sickle. But this should not be understood to mean that it could be compared to anything spatial or measurable; rather it moved like a sickle because, as it approached her, love at first drew back not bestowing itself as much as it had led her to understand it would, and as much as she did understand it would at that time; and this made her languish for more. (Again, the movement of the sickle was not something that could be compared to anything spatial or material because it was a reality perceptible only to her mind through the ineffable workings of divine grace.) Afterwards, Christ's faithful one was immediately filled with love and inexpressible contentment which, satisfactory as it was, nonetheless generated in her a hunger so unspeakably great that all her members dislocated. As a result of this vision, her soul was in a state of languor. What she wanted to see and feel was God, and not any creature. She did not speak nor could she make any words come out, but her soul spoke inwardly and cried out to God not to leave her languishing in such a death, for she regarded life as death. She also first called upon the Blessed Virgin, and then invoked and beseeched all the apostles to accompany her in kneeling before the Most High and implore him not to make her suffer this death, namely, the present life, but to enable her to attain the One she was feeling.

Vision of the Blessed Virgin and Christ in Glory

On another occasion Christ's faithful one said: My soul was elevated. I was not in prayer at that time, but had laid down to rest, for it was after a meal. So, not expecting it, my soul was suddenly elevated, and I saw the Blessed Virgin in glory. I had great delight in seeing a woman placed in such a position of nobility, glory, and dignity as was the Blessed Virgin, and in seeing her placed in the position of interceding for the human race. It likewise was an inexpressible delight for me to see her displaying such human concern and adorned with such indescribable virtues. While I was contemplating this spectacle, suddenly Christ in his glorified humanity appeared seated next to her. I perceived then how he had been crucified in his flesh, tormented and covered with opprobrium. And while I had an extraordinary perception of all the torments, injuries, humiliations, and defamations which he suffered, nonetheless for my part I was in no way grieved over these, rather they were a source of such delight that I cannot speak about it. I lost the power of speech and I thought I would die. The mere thought of not dying was a source of extreme pain for me, as well as the thought of not yet being able to attain this totally indescribable good which I had seen. This vision lasted without interruption for three days. It did not prevent me from eating or anything else, but I ate little and was continually lying down. I was stretched out on my bed and could not speak. And when God's name was mentioned in my presence I could not bear it because of the state of immense delight I was in.

A Plenitude, a Beauty ... the All Good

Once Christ's faithful one confessed herself to me, brother scribe, as was her wont, with such a perfect awareness of her sins and with such contrition and abundant tears from the beginning of her confession until almost the end, and with such honesty, that I wept from it, and my heart was firmly persuaded that even if the entire world were deceived, God would not permit that one so true and upright could be. I deliberated over this persuasion in my heart because, having heard such exceedingly great things from her, I marveled at them, for they had stirred some doubts in me and tested my credulity. The following night she was sick almost to the point of death, and it was a great struggle for her to come to the church of the friars the next morning. I celebrated Mass and gave her communion. After I had given her communion, before her departure, I pressed her to tell me if God had granted her a special grace. She responded as follows: Before receiving communion, just as I was about to do so, I was told: "Beloved, the All Good is within you, and you come to receive the All Good." And then it seemed to me that I saw almighty God. I, brother scribe, asked her if she had seen something with any form. She said she hadn't. But I pressed her further, and she responded: I saw a plenitude, a beauty wherein I saw the All Good. This vision came suddenly — it was the furthest thing from my mind — while I was praying, meditating, and confessing my sins before God. My prayer was that the communion I was about to receive be not for judgment over me but for mercy. Immediately and abruptly I heard the words which I have just related. Then I began to think: "If the All Good is already in me, why am I to receive him again?" An answer was immediately provided: "One does not exclude the other." And before entering the choir to receive communion, I had also been told the following: "The Son of God is on the altar according to his humanity and his divinity, and he is accompanied by a multitude of angels." Since I had a great desire to see him with the angels, as I had been told I would, I was then shown that beauty and plenitude of God I have already mentioned. Afterwards, when I approached the altar, in a similar fashion, I saw God, and I heard it said: "Thus you will stand before him in eternal life." She also said that he had called her "my beloved," and he often called her by this name.

The Savor of the Host

[...] She then added that recently when she receives communion, the host lingers in her mouth. She said that it does not have the taste of any known bread or meat. It has most certainly a meat taste, but one very different and most savory. I cannot find anything to compare it to. The host goes down very smoothly and pleasantly not crumbling into little pieces as it used to do. It disintegrates very quickly, she said, and does not stay hard as formerly. It goes down so smoothly that if I had not been told that one must swallow it right away, I would willingly hold it in my mouth for a great while. But at that moment, I also suddenly remember that I must swallow it right away. And as I do so, the body of Christ goes down with this unknown taste of meat. It goes down so smoothly that afterwards I do not need to drink any water. This is not the way it usually happens for me, for I usually have to make an effort to make sure that nothing of the host remains between my teeth. In this present experience, it goes down immediately, and when it descends into my body it produces in me a most pleasant sensation, and this can be detected outwardly because it makes me shake so violently that I must make a great effort to take the chalice.

Signs of the Certitude of God's Presence

[...] Christ's faithful one, responding to a question put to her concerning the Pilgrim, and another question which I, brother scribe, asked her, namely, whether the soul can be assured of possessing God in this life, replied that she knew that the Pilgrim had come into her soul, but did not know if she had granted him hospitality.

A) When he comes without being summoned.

I, brother scribe, asked how she knew that God had come into her soul, and she responded to my question with one of her own: "Does God come into the soul without being summoned by it to do so?" To this I replied: "I do believe that he does come in this fashion." Christ's faithful one in turn responded to this as follows: Sometimes God comes into the soul without being summoned, and when he does, he instills in the soul both fire and love, and sometimes a sweet feeling of his presence. The soul believes that this experience comes from God and delights in it. But it is still unaware that he himself is in the soul, that is, it does not perceive that he is in the soul, but is aware of the presence of his grace from which it takes delight.

B) When all fears are taken away.

The soul also experiences God's coming into it when it hears him speaking very sweetly to it, which greatly delights the soul, for it then feels his presence. But a doubt remains, even if it is a very small one, because the soul is not really certain that God is in it. It seems to me that this happens because of the ill-will or defect of the creature; or because it is God's will that the soul will not as yet be secure and certain of his presence. The soul nonetheless is assured that God is within it because it feels his presence in a different way than usual, with doubled intensity and with such divine fire and love that all the fears of soul and body are taken away. The soul speaks about these things, though it never heard them spoken by any mortal, and understands them with such great clarity that to be silent about them is painful. If it keeps silent, it does so out of deep concern not to displease love, and because it believes with the utmost certitude that these exceedingly lofty matters would not be understood — for when it does say something about them, it sees and experiences that it is not understood — and also because it does not want to say: "I myself experienced such lofty revelations" out of its deep concern not to displease love.

C) When the soul wants God perfectly.

She added that when sometimes, because of the great zeal that was hers for the salvation of her neighbor, she did say something about these revelations, she was reprimanded and told: "Sister, go back to Holy Scripture, for they say nothing about these revelations, and we do not understand you." Thus once when I was lying down, languishing from the experience of this excessive love, and I began to ask you if the soul could be assured of possessing God in this life, and I spoke to you about what I was feeling, you reprimanded me and referred me to the Scriptures. In this felt experience wherein the soul finds the certitude that God is within it, the soul is given the grace of wanting God so perfectly that everything in it is in true and not false harmony. False harmony exists when the soul says that it wants God but does not really mean it, because its desire for God is not true in everything, in every way, or in every respect. Its desire for God is true when all the members of the body are in harmony with the soul, and the soul in turn is in such harmony with the heart and with the entire body that it becomes one with them and responds as one for all of them. Then the soul truly wants God, and this desire is granted to it through grace. Hence when the soul is told: "What do you want?" It can respond: "I want God." God then tells it, "I am the one making you feel that desire." Until it reaches this point, the soul's desire is not true or integral. This form of desire is granted to the soul by a grace by which it knows that God is within it, and that it is in companionship with God. This gift is to have a desire, now a unified one, in which it feels that it loves God in a way analogous to the true love with which God has loved us. The soul feels God merging with it and becoming its companion.

D) When the soul sees God more clearly than a person can see another person.

In the fourth way, the soul is granted the gift to see God in the following fashion. It is first told by God: "Look at me." And then the soul sees him taking shape within itself and it sees him more clearly than a person can see another person, for the eyes of the soul, in this experience, see a fullness of God's presence of which I am not able to speak. What they see of this presence, which renders one speechless, is a spiritual and not a material reality. The soul delights in this vision, and this is an evident sign for it that God is within it. The soul then cannot look at anything else except that vision, and it fills the soul with God's incomparable presence. This beholding, in which the soul cannot look at anything else, is so deep and so profound that it grieves me not to be able to say anything about it. This vision is not tangible or imaginable, but something ineffable. In still many other ways does the soul know that God comes into it, ways which cannot be doubted. I will now speak of two of these.

E) When there is perfect harmony between the body and the soul.

One way consists of an unction which suddenly so revitalizes the soul and renders every member of the body so docile and in harmony with it that nothing can touch it or offend it;

and no event great or small can disturb it. In this experience the soul feels and hears God speaking to it. Furthermore, in this great and totally ineffable unction, the soul knows with the utmost certitude and clarity that God is within it, and that no saint in paradise nor any angel could cause this experience. But this experience is so ineffable that it grieves me not to be able to come up with anything to compare it to. God forgive me, for I would so much like to say all I know about it, but I would desire to do so only to manifest his goodness, if it so pleased him.

F) When God embraces the soul with indescribable love.

Still another way in which the soul knows that God is within it is by an embrace which God bestows upon the soul. Never has a mother embraced her son with such love, nor can anyone else on this earth be imagined who embraces with a love that nears the indescribable love with which God embraces the soul. He presses it to himself with such tenderness and such love that I think that no one on earth who has not had this experience can believe it. Since I, brother scribe, resisted her on this point — for I found it hard to believe — Christ's faithful one responded: "One could perhaps believe something of it but not its full expression." This embrace of God sets ablaze a fire within the soul with which the whole soul burns Christ. It also produces a light so great that the soul understands the fullness of God's goodness, which it experiences in itself, and which is, moreover, much greater than the soul's experience of it. The effect then of this fire within the soul is to render it certain and secure that Christ is within it. And yet, what we have said is nothing in comparison to what this experience really is.

G) When it grants hospitality to the Pilgrim [...]

Christ's faithful one also told me, brother scribe, that in all the cases above, the soul knows that God has come into it. But, she added, we haven't said anything yet about how the soul grants hospitality to him. Everything we have said thus far comes nowhere near to expressing what the soul knows when it grants hospitality to the Pilgrim. Christ's faithful one went on: When my soul knows that it has given hospitality to the Pilgrim, it reaches such a level of understanding of the goodness of God, indeed of his infinite goodness, that when I return to myself, I know with the utmost certainty that the more one feels God, the less is one able to say anything about him, for the very fact of feeling something of this infinite and unutterable Good renders one incapable of speaking about it. Since I resisted her on this point, Christ's faithful one elaborated: Would that when you go to preach you could understand, as I understood when I knew I had given hospitality to the Pilgrim. For then you would be absolutely unable to say anything about God; and neither could anyone else. Then I would like to come to you and tell you: "Brother, say something to me, now, about God." And you wouldn't be able to say anything at all or come up with any thought about God, his infinite goodness being so far beyond anything you could possibly say or think. In this state, I must add, the soul doesn't lose its self-awareness or the body the use of any of its senses; rather, one is in complete possession of oneself. And thus if you had attained this state, you would then say to the people with total self-assurance: "Go with God, because about God I can say nothing."

Angela's Eyes Shine like Candles

[...] [Angela's companion] told me that once while she and Angela were walking together along a road, the countenance of Christ's faithful one became white and radiant, then ruddy and joyful, and her eyes grew large and shone so brilliantly that she no longer seemed herself. This same companion also told me: "When I saw Angela in this state I was filled with sadness and feared that someone, a man or a woman, would meet us and notice her in this state. I told Angela, 'Why don't you at least try to cover your face? Your eyes seem to shine like candles.'" This companion, because she was shy and very simple, and still did not know all the gifts of grace Angela had been granted, then began to lament and beat her breasts with her fists, and said to Christ's faithful one: "Tell me why this is happening to you? Try to get out of sight or hide yourself somewhere, for we cannot walk around if you are in such a state." Out of her simplicity and ignorance, she then cried out: "Woe is me, what are we going to do?" Christ's faithful one, for her part, trying to console and reassure her, told her: "Do not fear, for even if we meet someone, God will help us." This happened not only once but so many times that her companion said she could not count them.

Sixth Supplementary Step

The Horrible Darkness

[...] Christ's faithful one told me, brother scribe, that she thought that the bodily ailments she endured were beyond description, and the ailments and sufferings of her soul were even more beyond any kind of comparison. In short, concerning the sufferings of the body, I heard her say that there was not one part of her body which had not suffered horribly.

The Torments of the Soul

Concerning the torments of the soul which demons afflicted upon her, she found herself incapable of finding any other comparison than that of a man hanged by the neck who, with his hands tied behind him and his eyes blindfolded, remains dangling on the gallows and yet lives, with no help, no support, no remedy, swinging in the empty air. She added that the demons pushed her to despair even more cruelly than this.[...] Christ's faithful one said: I perceive that demons hold my soul in a state of suspension; just as a hanged man has nothing to support him, so my soul does not seem to have any supports left. The virtues of my soul are undermined, while my soul sees it and knows it and watches it happening. And when it perceives all its virtues being subverted and departing, and it can do nothing to prevent this process, the pain and the anger that it feels pushes it to such a point of despair that at times it cannot weep and at other times it weeps inconsolably. There are even times when I am so overwhelmed with rage that I can hardly restrain from tearing myself apart, while at other moments I cannot refrain from horribly beating myself and I raise welts on my head and various parts of my body. When my soul sees all its virtues fall and leave, then it is overcome with fear and grief. It wails and cries out to God repeatedly and unceasingly: "My son, my son, do not abandon me, my son!"

The Bodily Ailments

Christ's faithful one also said that there was no part of her body which was not beaten and afflicted by demons. Because of the horrible nature of these afflictions, she asserted that the bodily ailments she suffered, like those of the soul, were beyond description. She also added that in this state all her past vices were revived, and even though this was only temporary, it caused her great torment. Even vices which she never knew existed entered her body, and though, likewise, these did not last, they too caused her great torment. And when these past vices were put to death again, she found consolation in her awareness that she had been handed over to many demons and they were responsible for the reawakening of these past dead vices as well as the addition of unknown ones.

Then, remembering that God was afflicted, despised, and poor while on earth, she desired that all her ills and afflictions be doubled. Christ's faithful one also said: While I am in this most horrible darkness caused by demons it seems to me that there is nothing I can hope for. That darkness is terrible; vices which I knew to be dead are reawakened from the outside by demons, and along with those, some vices which had never been there before come alive in my soul. My body (which nonetheless suffers less than my soul) experiences such burning in three places — the shameful parts — that I used to apply material fire to quench the other fire, until you forbade me to do so. When I am in that darkness I think I would prefer to be burned than to suffer such afflictions. I even cry out for death to come in whatever form God would grant it. I beseech him to send me to hell without delay. "Since you have abandoned me," I tell him, "make an end to it now and completely submerge me into the abyss."

Struggle Between Humility and Pride

[...] Christ's faithful one told me, brother scribe, the following: A certain kind of humility was in continual conflict in my soul with a certain kind of especially vexing pride. It is humility because I perceive myself as fallen from every good and devoid of every virtue and grace. In this state, I perceive myself as so full of sins and defects that it is impossible for me to imagine that God could henceforth ever wish to have mercy on me. I perceive myself as the house of the devil, a worker for and a dupe of demons, their daughter even. I perceive myself devoid of rectitude and virtue, indeed, worthy only of the lowest part in hell. This, I want to specify, is not the same humility that is sometimes mine, which brings contentment to my soul and makes me come to the awareness of the goodness of God. Rather, this humility is accompanied with countless ill effects. It gives me the impression that my soul is surrounded by demons and makes me aware of the defects of my body and soul. I am completely closed off from God in such a way that I cannot recall God's presence, have any remembrance of him, or even be aware that he is the one who allows this to happen. I see myself as damned, but I am in no way preoccupied with this damnation; rather, what concerns me and grieves me most is having offended my creator, for I do not want to offend him or to have offended him for all the good or evil that can be named. Perceiving my innumerable offenses, I fight with all my strength against the demons so that I may conquer and prevail over the aforesaid vices and sins. But there is no way I can do so. I cannot find any ford to cross to safety, not even a small window through which I could escape; I find no remedy which could be of any help to me. It weighs heavily on me to have fallen so low.

Pride, the Final Assault

After this, pride begins its assault, and its effect is to make me full of anger, sadness, bitterness, and conceit. I even derive extreme bitterness from the favors God granted to me in the past. Now when I remember them, I derive no comfort from the memory. Now these gifts offend me, and to my astonishment and dismay, I even entertain the conviction that there never was any true virtue in me. Nor do I see any reason that God could have allowed virtue to exist in me. Every good is so closed off and hidden from me that I become full of anger, sadness, bitterness, conceit, and affliction beyond what I can say. And even if all the consolers, all the wise of the world, and all the saints in paradise would try to offer words of solace and would promise me every imaginable good and consolation, and even if God himself would speak to me (unless he were to alter the present state of my soul or his mode of operation), I would draw no consolation or healing from it; nor would I believe anything of what they said. Even more, all their words would only serve to increase my ills, anger, bewilderment, sadness, and pain more than I can say. In exchange for these torments and in order that God might take them away, I would willingly choose and would prefer to undergo all the afflictions, ailments, and pains which have existed in the bodies of everyone at once. I think these would be less than the above torments. Finally, in exchange for them I would regard every imaginable kind of martyrdom as consolation.

How this Struggle Purifies the Soul

These torments, which were frequent, began sometime before the pontificate of Pope Celestine and lasted for more than two years. Toward the end of this period I was not fully and entirely liberated from them; I still felt some of their outer effects but not their inner ones. But now that I have entered another state, I am aware that through this struggle with the aforesaid humility and pride extreme purgation and purification have taken place in my soul. I have realized that without humility no one can be saved. The greater one's humility, the greater is the perfection of the soul. I have become aware also that caught in this struggle between humility and pride, the soul has passed through fire and undergone martyrdom. The truth of this humility is such that the soul truly becomes aware of its own offenses and defects as they are brought to light through punishment, martyrdom, and purgation by the said pride and demons. For this reason, I also became aware that the more a soul is laid low, abased, impoverished, and thoroughly humiliated, the more it is prepared, purged, and purified for a greater elevation. For the extent of the soul's elevation corresponds to the extent of its humiliation and abasement. The matters mentioned above are a beautiful illustration of this truth.

Seventh Supplementary Step

The Most Wonderful Step of All: the Light, the Beauty, and the Fullness of God

[...] Christ's faithful one said the following: Once my soul was elevated, and I saw the light, the beauty, and the fullness that is in God in a way that I had never seen before in so great a manner. I did not see love there, I then lost the love which was mine and was made nonlove.

The Dazzling Darkness of God

Afterward, I saw him in a darkness, and in a darkness precisely because the good that he is, is far too great to be conceived or understood. Indeed, anything conceivable or understandable does not attain this good or even come near it. My soul was then granted a most certain faith, a secure and most firm hope, a continual security about God which took away all my fear. In this good, which is seen in the darkness, I recollected myself totally. I was made so sure of God that in no way can I ever entertain any doubts about him or of my possession of him. Of this I have the utmost certitude. And in this most efficacious good seen in this darkness now resides my most firm hope, one in which I am totally recollected and secure.

Standing or Lying in the midst of the Trinity

[...] On the other hand, God draws me to himself. But if I say that he draws me to himself with gentleness or love or anything which can be named, conceived, or imagined, that is completely false; for he does not draw me by anything which can be named or conceived by even the wisest in the world. Even if I say that it is the All Good which draws me, I destroy it. For in this state, it seems to me that I am standing or lying in the midst of the Trinity, and that is what I see with such darkness. This draws me more than anything else I have experienced so far, more than any good ever spoken of before. So much more so that there is nothing to compare to it. Everything I say now about it seems to say nothing or to be badly said.

Mystical Marriage

When I am in that darkness I do not remember anything about anything human. I see all and I see nothing. As what I have spoken of withdraws and stays with me, I see the God-man. He draws my soul with great gentleness and he sometimes says to me: "You are I and I am you." I see, then, those eyes and that face so gracious and attractive as he leans to embrace me. In short, what proceeds from those eyes and that face is what I said that I saw in that previous darkness which comes from within, and which delights me so that I can say nothing about it. When I am in the God-man my soul is alive. And I am in the God-man much more than in the other vision of seeing God with darkness. The soul is alive in that vision concerning the God-man. The vision with darkness, however, draws me so much more that there is no comparison. On the other hand, I am in the God-man almost continually. It began in this continual fashion on a certain occasion when I was given the assurance that there was no intermediary between God and myself. Since that time there has not been a day or a night in which I did not continually experience this joy of the humanity of Christ.

The Bed to Rest On

At this moment, my desire is to sing and praise:
I praise you God my beloved;
I have made your cross my bed.
For a pillow or cushion,
I have found poverty,
and for other parts of the bed,
suffering and contempt to rest on.

When I, brother scribe, asked her for a better explanation of what she had said, Christ's faithful one added: This bed is my bed to rest on because on it Christ was born, lived, and died. Even before man sinned, God the Father loved this bed and its company (poverty, suffering, and contempt) so much that he granted it to his Son. And, in concord with the Father, the Son wanted to lie in this bed and continued to love it. This is why this bed is my bed, namely, the cross where Christ suffered in his body and much more in his soul, and on it I have placed myself and I have found my rest. On this bed I believe I die and through this bed I believe I am saved. I cannot describe the joy which I expect from those hands and feet and the marks from the nails which pierced them on that bed. Humming, I say to the Son of the Blessed Mary: "What I feel there are no words for; what I see I never want to depart from. Because for me to live is to die. Oh, draw me then to yourself!"

The Justice of God's Judgments

[...] Nothing gives me such a complete knowledge of God as my recognition of him through his judgments. At night or in the morning, when I recite a litany, praying to God as follows: "Lord deliver me by your coming, and deliver me by your nativity, and your passion," there is nothing that delights me more than when I reach the invocation in which I proclaim joyfully and confidently: "By your holy judgments deliver me, O Lord." Christ's faithful one added: The reason why I proclaim with such joy and confidence to God, "By your holy judgments deliver me," is because I do not recognize God's goodness more in one good and holy person, or even in many good and holy people, than in one or many who are damned. This profound truth was shown to me only once, but the memory and the joy of it never leave me. Even if all the other truths of faith were shaken, I would still be sure of this one, namely, the justice of God's judgments. What depths are found there! All of them serve to benefit the good, for every soul which has — or will have — the knowledge of these judgments and their depth will reap benefits in everything that happens to them from their awareness of this attribute of God.

Every Previous State Is Put to Sleep

[...] I was and am now drawn out of everything I had previously experienced and had taken such delight in: the life and humanity of Christ; the consideration of that very deep companionship which the Father from eternity in his love had bestowed on his Son (in which I had taken such deep delight), namely, the contempt, the suffering, and the poverty experienced by the Son of God; and the cross as bed to rest on. I was also drawn out of the vision of God in the darkness in which I used to take such delight. Every previous state was put to sleep so tenderly and sweetly that I could not tell it was happening. I could only recall that now I do not have these experiences. For in the cross of Christ in which I used to take such delight, so as to make it my place of rest and my bed, I find nothing; in the poverty of the Son of God, I find nothing; and in everything that could be named, I find nothing. In all these totally ineffable workings which take place in the soul, God initially makes his presence felt in the soul through these ineffable workings. Then he manifests himself by disclosing himself to the soul and by bestowing ever greater gifts on it, accompanied by ever greater clarity and ineffable certitude. The two ways that he initially makes his presence felt are the following.

God Is Present in All That Exists Good or Bad

In the first mode, God presents himself in the inmost depths of my soul. I understand not only that he is present, but also how he is present in every creature and in everything that has being, in a devil and a good angel, in heaven and hell, in good deeds and in adultery or homicide, in all things finally which exist or have some degree of being, whether beautiful or ugly. She further said: I also understand the he is no less present in a devil than a good angel. Therefore, while I am in this truth, I take no less delight in seeing or understanding his presence in a devil or in an act of adultery than I do in a good angel or in a good deed. This mode of divine presence in my soul has become almost habitual. Moreover, this mode of God's presence illuminates my soul with such great truth and bestows on it such divine graces that when my soul is in this mode it cannot commit any offense, and it receives an abundance of divine gifts. Because of this understanding of God's presence my soul is greatly humiliated and ashamed of its sins. It is also granted deep wisdom, great divine consolation, and joy.

The Joy of Eternal Life

Another mode of God's being present to my soul is much more special and quite different from the previous one; and the joy that he grants to it is also different, for in this state he gathers me totally into himself. God produces in my soul many divine workings accompanied by much greater graces, and there is so deep and ineffable an abyss that this presence of God alone, without any other gifts, is that good that the saints enjoy in eternal life. Of these gifts of Paradise, some saints have more, others less. And these gifts — even though I cannot find words to describe them, for my words blaspheme and make hash of what they should express — I affirm that they are expansions of the soul through which it is rendered more capable of possessing God.

Nothing Can Explain God

And immediately upon presenting himself to the soul, God likewise discloses himself and expands the soul and gives it gifts and consolations which the soul has never before experienced, and which are far more profound than earlier ones. In this state, the soul is drawn out of all darkness and granted a greater awareness of God than I would have thought possible. This awareness is of such clarity, certitude, and abysmal profundity that there is no heart in the world that can ever in any way understand it or even conceive it. Even my own heart cannot think about it by itself, or ever return to it to understand or even conceive anything about it. This state occurs only when God, as a gift, elevates the soul to himself, for no heart by itself can in any way expand itself to attain it. Therefore, there is absolutely nothing that can be said about this experience, for no words can be found or invented to express or explain it, no expansion of thought or mind can possibly reach to those things; they are so far beyond everything — for there is nothing which can explain God. I repeat there is absolutely nothing which can explain God. Christ's faithful one affirmed with utmost certitude and wanted it understood that there is absolutely nothing which can explain God.

The Secrets of the Scriptures

Holy Scripture, she added, is so sublime that there is no one in the world wise enough, not even anyone with learning and spirit, who would not find it totally beyond their capacity to understand Scripture fully; still, they babble something about it. But of these ineffable workings which are produced in the soul when God discloses himself to it, nothing at all can be said or babbled. Because my soul is often elevated into the secret levels of God and sees the divine secrets, I am able to understand how the Scriptures were written; how they are made easy and difficult; how they seem to say something and contradict it; how some derive no profit from them; how those who do not observe them are damned and Scripture is fulfilled in them; and how others who observe them are saved by them. I see all this from above. Thus when I return to myself after perceiving these divine secrets, I can say some words with security about them, but then I speak entirely from outside the experience, and say words that come nowhere near describing the divine workings that are produced in my soul. My statements about them ruin the reality they represent. This is why I say that I blaspheme in speaking about them.

The Chamber in the Soul Where the Complete Truth Resides

[...] Even if at times I can still experience outwardly some little sadness and joy, nonetheless there is in my soul a chamber in which no joy, sadness, or enjoyment from any virtue, or delight over anything that can be named, enters. This is where the All Good, which is not any particular good, resides, and it is so much the All Good that there is no other good. Although I blaspheme by speaking about it — and I speak about it so badly because I cannot find words to express it — I nonetheless affirm that in this manifestation of God I discover the complete truth. In it, I understand and possess the complete truth that is in heaven and in hell, in the entire world, in every place, in all things, in every enjoyment in heaven and in every creature. And I see all this so truly and certainly that no one could convince me otherwise. Even if the whole world were to tell me otherwise, I would laugh it to scorn.

The Vision of "The One Who Is"

Furthermore, I saw the One who is and how he is the being of all creatures. I also saw how he made me capable of understanding those realities I have just spoken about better than when I saw them in that darkness which used to delight me so. Moreover, in that state I see myself as alone with God, totally cleansed, totally sanctified, totally true, totally upright, totally certain, totally celestial in him. And when I am in that state, I do not remember anything else. On one occasion, while I was in that state, God told me: "Daughter of divine wisdom, temple of the beloved, beloved of the beloved, daughter of peace, in you rests the entire Trinity; indeed, the complete truth rests in you, so that you hold me and I hold you."

The Soul Experiences its Own Presentation Before God

[...] During that period when that unspeakable manifestation of God was occurring in my soul, one day, on the feast of St. Mary of Candlemas, while blessed candles were being distributed for the celebration of the presentation of the Son of God in the temple, and at the very moment when this unspeakable manifestation of God was taking place, my soul experienced its own presentation. And it saw itself so noble and elevated that, henceforth, I cannot conceive or even imagine that my soul or even the souls in paradise could be or are endowed with such nobility. My soul then could not comprehend itself. If the soul, which is created, finite, and circumscribed, cannot comprehend itself, will it not be far less able to comprehend God, the creator, who is immense and infinite? My soul, then, immediately presented itself before God with the utmost assurance and without any fear. This presentation was accompanied with greater delight than I have ever experienced, with a new and most excellent joy, and with new miracles, so much so that I cannot imagine that my soul ever experienced anything so miraculous, so clear, and so new. Such was this encounter with God. In this encounter I simultaneously perceived and experienced both that previous unspeakable manifestation of God to my soul, and this new manifestation of my soul and its presentation to God. In this I found new delights different from all previous delights, and I was told most high words which I do not want to be written.

Nothing Separates Angela from God

After this, when I returned to myself, I discovered that I was glad to suffer every injury and pain for God, and that nothing anyone could say or do could henceforth separate me from him. And I cried out: "Lord what can henceforth separate me from you?" In response, I was told that there was nothing that could separate me from God. Furthermore, I delighted in the thought of my death. One cannot imagine the delight that is mine when I think of the day of my death. After everything written above, Christ's faithful one also told me, brother scribe, that she had heard God speaking to her in words too wonderful to relate. She was told that this unspeakable good mentioned above is the same good and none other than that which the saints enjoy in eternal life, but there the experience of it is different. In eternal life the least saint has more of it than can be given to any soul in this life before the death of the body. Christ's faithful one said that she understood this. Thanks be to God always. Amen.

God Puts His Seal on Everything That Has Been Written

After I, brother scribe, had written almost everything which can be found in this small book, I asked and requested Christ's faithful one to beseech God and pray that if I had written anything false or superfluous he would, in his mercy, reveal it and show it to her, so that we would both know the truth from God himself. Christ's faithful one responded b saying: Before you made this request, I myself often asked God to make known to me if in what I said or what you wrote there was any word of untruth or anything superfluous, so that I could at least confess myself of it. God answered me that everything I had said and you had written was completely true and contained nothing false or superfluous. She also told me that I had tempered what God had told her for there was much that he had told her which I could have put into writing but did not. God, she said, even told me: "Everything which has been written is in conformity with my will and comes from me, that is, issues forth from me." Then he added: "I will put my seal to it." Since I did not understand what he meant by these words "I will put my seal to it," he clarified these words by saying; "I will sign it."

Selections from the Instructions

Instruction II

The Weapons of Love

[...] The weapons by which good love ought to be regulated are found and transmitted through transformations which take place in the soul. There are three kinds of transformations: sometimes the soul is transformed to obey God's will; sometimes it is with God; at other times it is within God and God is within the soul. The first transformation occurs when the soul strives to imitate the works of the suffering God-man in whom is manifested God's will. The second transformation occurs when the soul is united with God, feels deeply the consolations of God's presence, and can express these with words and thoughts. The third occurs when the soul, by a most perfect union, is transformed within God, and God is within the soul; then it feels and tastes God's presence in such a sublime way that it is beyond words and conception. The first transformation has nothing to do with the type of love we are considering. The second suffices to regulate love if it is truly alive in the soul. The third is the most efficacious. In the third transformation (and even in the second, but not so perfectly), the soul is infused with the grace of a wisdom by which it knows how to regulate the love of God and neighbor. The soul then knows how to harmonize the sentiments, sweetnesses, and fervor that it receives from God so wisely that love is stabilized and can persevere in what it undertakes without any outward show of laughter, bodily movements, or gestures. Likewise in love of one's neighbor or friends the soul brings to it such wisdom and maturity that it expresses love when it is appropriate, and does not when it is not appropriate. The reason for this that while God is unchangeable, the soul is not; but the more the soul is united to God, the less it is subject to change. From such a union the soul acquires wisdom, maturity, depth, discernment, and enlightenment, and armed with these it knows how to regulate the love of God and neighbor so well that it cannot be deceived or fall into disorder. Whoever does not feel infused with such wisdom should never extend special love or heartfelt affection toward any man or woman, for even if it is done for God's sake and with the best intentions, one runs the risk of encountering the dangers inherent to love. One should never bind oneself to another until one has first learned to separate oneself from others.

The Perils of Love

[...] There are many who believe themselves to be in a state of love who are actually in a state of hatred. And there are many who believe they possess God while in reality they love the flesh, the world, and the devil. Hence some love God so that he will protect them from sickness, bodily ailments, and temporal dangers. Such persons even love themselves in such a disorderly way that they treat their bodies as though they were souls and gods. They even love material things to put these at the service of the gods they have made of their bodies. They love their friends and relatives inordinately as a way of benefitting from them and being honored by them. They love persons devoted to the spiritual life not for their goodness but to cover themselves with the mantle of their holiness. Because such a love is not pure, its fruit is the flesh with all its carnal and spiritual vices. They love to possess special talents such as knowing how to read and sing well so that they might please others. They love to possess great learning so that they can persuade others not through love but by force of reason and arrogantly correct others so as to appear important. There are others who believe they love God, and they do love him, but their love is infirm and imperfect. They love God, for instance, so that he will remit their sins, preserve them from hell, and grant them the glory of Paradise. They love God so that he will preserve their goodness, and so that they will not offend him any longer and not lose Paradise. They love God to receive consolations and sweetnesses from him. They love God to be loved by him. They even love their friends and relatives with a spiritual love because they desire to be spiritual and good and they desire this for their own sake, to gain honor and profit from it. Those who are literate love God to receive from him the meaning, knowledge, and understanding of the Scriptures. Those who are illiterate desire to have the capacity to speak usefully and spiritually for the benefit of others so that they may be more loved and more honored. They love spiritual persons so that they may be considered one of them and be loved by them for their own spiritual benefit and honor. They even love poverty, humility, obedience, contempt, and other virtues because they wish to excel in these over others and because they hope that no one can match them in perfection. They wish to have no equal in the ways of the spirit. In this they resemble Lucifer's sin, for he too did not want anyone to achieve his perfection. There are others who lavish praise on all, whether they be spiritual persons or not, because they wish to enjoy a universal reputation of holiness and be praised by all, good and bad alike, for their holiness.

The Highest Form of Love

[...] The perfect and highest form of love, one without defects, is the one in which the soul is drawn out of itself and led into the vision of the being of God. For when the soul is so drawn out of itself and led into this vision it perceives how every creature has its being from the one who is the supreme being; how all things and all that exists come to be through the supreme being; how God is indeed the only one who has being, and that nothing has being unless it comes from him. The soul drawn out of itself and led into this vision derives from it an ineffable wisdom, one that is deep and mature. In this vision, the soul discovers that only what is best comes from the supreme being and it cannot deny this, for it sees in truth that all things that are from him are excellently made; things are done badly when we have destroyed those things he made. This vision of the supreme being also stirs up in the soul a love corresponding and proportionate to its object, for it teaches us to love everything which receives existence from the supreme being. It likewise teaches us to love everything which has being, that is, every creature, rational and non-rational with the supreme being's own love. It teaches us to love rational creatures, especially those we know are loved and cherished by him. When the soul sees the supreme being stoop down lovingly towards creatures, it does likewise.

Instruction III

The Necessity of Prayer

[...] No one can be saved without divine light. Divine light causes us to begin and to make progress, and it leads us to the summit of perfection. Therefore if you want to begin and to receive this divine light, pray. If you have begun to make progress and want this light to be intensified within you, pray. And if you have reached the summit of perfection, and want to be super-illumined so as to remain in that state, pray. If you want faith, pray. If you want hope, pray. If you want charity, pray. If you want poverty, pray. If you want obedience, pray. If you want chastity, pray. If you want humility, pray. If you want meekness, pray. If you want fortitude, pray. If you want some virtue, pray. And pray in this fashion, namely, always reading the Book of Life, that is, the life of the God-man Jesus Christ, whose life consisted of poverty, pain, contempt, and true obedience. Once you have entered this way and are making progress in it, tribulations, temptations from demons, the world, and the flesh, will plague you in many ways and afflict you horribly; but if you want to overcome these, pray. And when the soul wants to improve its prayer, it must enter into it with a cleansed mind and body, and with pure and right intention. Its task is also to turn evil into good, and not, as many of the wicked do, convert good into evil. A soul thus exercised in cleansing itself goes with greater confidence to confession to have its sins washed away. And so that nothing impure may remain, it puts itself to a kind of scrutiny. It enters into prayer and examines the good and evil it has done. As it tries to determine the intentions behind the good things it has done, it discovers how in its fasts, prayers, tears, and all its other good deeds, it has behaved deceitfully, that is, inadequately and defectively. You are not to behave, therefore, like the wicked, but rather confess your sins diligently and grieve over them, for it is in confession that the soul is cleansed. After this, you are to return to prayer and not let yourself become preoccupied with anything else. As a result, you begin to feel the presence of God more fully than usual because your palate is more disposed to savor God's presence than before. It is through prayer, then, that one will be given the most powerful light to see God and self.

Be on Guard Against the False Teachers of Prayer

Beware of giving yourself to another unless first you learn to separate yourself from others. Beware also of those who flatter you with sweet words and seek to make themselves especially attractive to you by what they say, and make a show of their revelations, because these are the snares of the wicked who try to lure others after them. Beware also of those who have merely the appearance of holiness and of good works, lest they drag you along their way. Beware also of your own fervor, that is, the spirit which accompanies this fervor; before following its lead, look, look again, examine it and determine its origins, its means, and its end. Follow its lead only to the extent that it corresponds to the way of the Book of Life and no further.

Temptations in Prayer

[...] Be careful not to give way to your enemies, who are continually watching you. For you will yield to your enemies if you stop praying. The more you are tempted, the more you should persevere in prayer. And by the very fact that you persevere in your prayers, you put yourself in a position to be tempted. Must not gold be purified and melted down? But by the very perseverance of your prayers you will be freed from temptations. Finally, it is through prayer that you will be enlightened, liberated, cleansed, and united with God.

Prayer, the Manifestation of God and Self

The purpose of prayer is nothing other than to manifest God and self. And this manifestation of God and self leads to a state of perfect and true humility. For this humility is attained when the soul sees God and self. It is in this profound state of humility, and from it, that divine grace deepens and grows in the soul. The more divine grace deepens humility in the soul, the more divine grace can grow in this depth of humility. The more divine grace grows, the deeper the soul is grounded, and the more it is settled in a state of true humility. Through perseverance in true prayer, divine light and grace increase, and these always make the soul grow deep in humility as it reads, as has been said, the life of Jesus Christ, God and man. I cannot conceive anything greater than the manifestation of God and self. But this discovery, that is, this manifestation of God and self, is the lot only of those legitimate sons of God who have devoted themselves to true prayer.

The Three Kinds of Prayer

[...] There are three kinds of prayer; bodily, mental, and supernatural. Divine wisdom is most orderly and it imposes its order on all things. Through its ineffable wisdom it has ordained that one does not attain mental prayer unless one has first passed through bodily prayer, and likewise, one does not attain supernatural prayer unless one has first passed through bodily and mental prayer. Divine wisdom also wills and has ordained that the canonical hours be said at the hours assigned for each one of them unless one is totally unable to do so because of some serious bodily ailment or because one is so absorbed in a state of mental or supernatural prayer and experiencing such joy in that state that one is totally speechless. Divine wisdom likewise teaches that when possible the hours should be said with the mind at rest and, as is fitting, in solitude, with the body in a recollected state. The more you pray the more you will be enlightened; and the more you are enlightened, the more deeply and exaltedly you will see the supreme good and what this supreme good consists of; the deeper and more perfect your vision, the more you will love; the more you love, the more you will delight in what you see; the more you find delight, the more you will understand and be made capable of understanding. Afterwards, you will come to the fullness of light because you will understand that you cannot understand.

The Path of Poverty

[...] It was on the path of poverty that the first man fell, and on the same path the second man, Christ, God and man, raised us up. The worst poverty is that of ignorance. Adam fell because of his ignorance; and all those who have fallen or are falling do so though ignorance. This is why it is fitting that the sons of God should rise and be restored through the opposite kind of poverty.

Blessed Francis, Example of True Poverty

[...] What a perfect example is given to us by our glorious father, blessed Francis, who possessed the ineffable light of the truest poverty! He was so filled, and more than filled, with this light, that he opened up a very special way and showed it to us all. I cannot think of any saint who demonstrated to me more remarkably than he did the way found in the Book of Life, the model being the life of the God-man, Jesus Christ. I know no other saint who more remarkably set himself to follow this way. He set himself with such determination along that path that his eyes never left it, and the effects could plainly be seen in his body. And because he set himself with such total determination to follow this path, he was filled to overflowing with the highest wisdom, a wisdom which he filled and continues to fill the whole world.

Teachings of the Blessed Francis

[...] There are two things which our blessed and glorious father Francis taught us in a remarkable way. One is to recollect ourselves in God, that is, to recollect our whole soul within the divine infinity. He was so filled to overflowing with the

Holy Spirit that the grace of that Spirit animated all his works and actions. The second lesson blessed Francis taught us was poverty, suffering, contempt, and true obedience. He was poverty personified, inside and out. He lived in this way and persevered in it to the end. Everything that Jesus, God and man, despised, he despised most perfectly. Everything that Jesus, God and man, loved, he loved most intensely and supremely. With inexpressible perfection he followed in the footsteps of Jesus in order to become conformed to him as much as he could in all things.

Instruction VII

Advice on Pastoral Ministry

[...] When one of you preaches, hears confessions, or gives counsel, he should not keep his mind on creatures, but on the Creator. Do not behave like fools, for whatever the fool has his eye on, there is his whole heart. When you come across flatterers, men or women, who tell you: "Brother, your words have converted me to penance," do not pay any attention to them but rather turn to the Creator and thank him for this blessing. There are many preachers of falsehoods whose preaching is full of greed, and out of greed they preach for honors, money, and fame. My beloved sons, I wish with all my heart that you preach the holy truth and that the book you rely on be the God-man. I do not tell you to give up your books, but that you should always be willing to do this, whether you keep them or abandon them. I don't want you to be like those who preach only with words of learning and dryly report the deeds of saints, but rather speak about them with the same divine savor as they had who performed these deeds. Those who have first preached well to themselves with this divine savor know how to preach well to others.

Instruction IX

How to Avoid Divisions

O you who are dearest to my soul, I desire for you what I desire for my companion and myself: that you always be of one mind and that there be no divisions among you. I desire that you have in your souls what leads from discord to unanimity, namely, becoming little. When you are little, you do not consider yourself self-sufficient because of your knowledge or natural abilities, but rather you are always inclined to acknowledge your defects and your miserable condition; you question yourself and contend against yourself so as to convince yourself of your defects and strive to correct them. To be little also means that you are not a threat or a burden to others; nor are your words contentious, even if your life strikes a powerful blow to all those who are opposed to this littleness. This is what I desire from you, my dearest ones, that by following this way of littleness and poverty, disciplined zeal and compassion, your life may be, even when your tongue is silent, a clear mirror for those who wish to follow this way, and a sharp-edged sword against the enemies of truth.

Instruction XIV

Importance of Knowledge of God and Self

Do not be surprised, my dearest sons, if I have not answered the several letters you have written to me. It is because I have been bound to God that I have not been able to write to you or to any others, nor could I give you any spiritual advice except the very ordinary words which follow. There are only two things in the world that I find pleasure in speaking about, namely, knowledge of God and self, and remaining continually in one's cell and never leaving it. If you leave your cell, you should strive to return to it with sorrow and true contrition. I believe that anyone who does not know how to stay put and remain in a cell ought not to go anywhere; it is not for them to seek out any other kind of good, and they ought not to probe into things which are above them. O my dearest sons, of what use are revelations, visions, feelings of God's presence, sweetnesses from him? Of what use are gifts of wisdom, elevations? Of what use even is contemplation? Indeed these are useless unless one has a true knowledge of God and self. That is why I am surprised that you expect letters from me, because I do not see that my letters or my words should or could console you, nor can I see how you could receive consolation from them unless they bestow upon you the kind of knowledge I am referring to. I find delight in speaking about this truth and nothing else; and silence has been imposed on me for everything else.

Instruction XV

The Cross of Christ and the Book of Life

O dearest son, if you wish to have the light of divine grace, and a heart free from all care, if you wish to curb all harmful temptations, and to be made perfect in the ways of God, do not tarry in running to the cross of Christ. Truly there is no other way for the sons of Christ to manage to find God, and having found him, to hold on to him, but in the life and the way of the suffering God and man which, as I have been in the habit of saying and which I reaffirm here, is the Book of Life, the reading of which no one can have access to except through continual prayer. Continual prayer elevates, illumines, and transforms the soul. Illumined by the light perceived in prayer, the soul sees clearly the way of Christ prepared and trodden by the feet of the Crucified; running along this way with an expanded heart, it not only distances itself from the weighty cares of the world but rises above itself to taste divine sweetness. Then it is set ablaze by divine fire. Thus illumined, elavated, and set ablaze, it is transformed into the God-man. All this is achieved by gazing on the cross in continual prayer.

Instruction XVII

The Birth of Christ in the Soul

O dearest one, part of my soul, I desire with my whole self that I might hear tell of you, that in your soul you desire, as the saints did, and do now, the Child who is soon to come and be born; and that he be born in your soul according to my desire. O dearest one to my soul, strive to know yourself, because, in truth, I do not believe that there is a greater virtue on earth. Try to rid yourself of every thought, every imagination harmful to your soul. Prepare yourself, as is my desire, to receive this Son about to be born, because, in truth, he is the one who will grant you knowledge of yourself. He will be the salvation of your soul, which I desire from the depths of my soul. And now may the Consoler console you, my soul!

Instruction XVIII

Perseverance in Prayer

I desire very much, my beloved son, that you be reborn and renewed. I also desire, my son, that you rid yourself completely of negligence and laziness. Furthermore, my son, I desire that you do not pray less, or keep vigils less often, or do any other good works any the less when divine grace is withdrawn from you than when it is in your possession.

It is a good thing and very acceptable to God, my son, if you pray, keep vigils, and perform other good works when the fervor of divine grace is with you, but it is altogether most pleasing and acceptable to God that, when divine grace is lacking or has been withdrawn from you, you do not pray less, keep vigils less often, or perform fewer good works. Act without grace just as you do when you have grace. Therefore, my son, if divine fervor or warmth impels you sometimes to pray, keep vigils, and devote yourself to spiritual discipline and exercises, then, when it is God's pleasure to withdraw this fervor or warmth from you — either because of some deficit in you or, which is most often, to amplify and increase his grace in you — strive to do your utmost not to pray less, or keep vigils less often, or be less persistent in doing good works. Even if you suffer tribulations or temptations, which serve to punish and purify the sons of God, and grace is taken from you, strive nonetheless not to pray less, keep vigils less often, or be less persistent in doing good works; likewise, strive to resist and fight against temptations just as much as ever, in order to overcome them. Thus by your continual prayers, vigils, tears, spiritual discipline and exercises, and every kind of importuning, may you at least force God to deign to restore to you at some time the fervor and warmth of his grace. Do your share, my son, for God will do his part well. Forced prayers, my son, are particularly pleasing to God.

Love of Angela for One of Her Spiritual Sons

When I gaze upon the uncreated God the experience is indescribable, most sweet, and consoling. Because of this, God, out of his indescribable kindness, makes me return to myself and turn and direct my gaze toward you. It seems to me that he shows me almost everything in you, inside and out, so that with a new and indescribable joy, I am made an entirely new person in you, so much so that I cannot take my eyes off you. You should know, my son, that this love is so intense that I ask him who produced it to moderate it, because it seems to me that I am no longer myself but you. This makes me say to myself: "I wonder to whom I am writing, since I am you and you are me." If you could see my heart, my son, you would be entirely bound to do what God wants, because my heart is God's heart and his mine. I am beginning to smile about you. I want that smile to grow, for it will have its fulfillment in Paradise.

Instruction XIX

Vision of Our Lady

On the morning of the feast of the Purification of the Blessed Virgin, I was in the church of the Friars Minor in Foligno when candles were being distributed. And I heard God telling me: "This is the hour when Our Lady came into the temple with her son." When my soul heard this I felt such great love welling in me that it is impossible for me to say or understand anything about it. Then my soul was elevated and saw Our Lady enter. I moved towards her with great reverence and fear. Our Lady totally reassured my soul, and she held forth her son to me and said: "Oh lover of my son, receive him." While saying these words she extended her arms and placed her son in my arms. He seemed to have his eyes closed as though asleep, and was wrapped in swaddling clothes. As if wearied from her journey, Our Lady sat down. Her gestures were so beautiful and gracious, her manner and behavior were likewise so gracious that it was exceedingly sweet and delightful for me to look at her and admire her. So much so that I turned again and again to look at the child, whom I held closely in my arms. And I likewise turned again and again to look at Our Lady herself, so beautiful was she to admire. Then, suddenly, the child was left naked in my arms. He opened his eyes and raised them and looked at me. I saw and felt such a love for me as he looked at me that I was completely overwhelmed. I brought my face close to his, and pressed mine to his. There was such a fire that emanated from the opening and raising of the eyes of that child, who remained naked in my arms, and the effect on me of this child and his opening his eyes in that way was a benefit so totally unspeakable that although I felt it, I can in no way speak about it.

Angela Offers Herself and Her Spiritual Sons to God

Then suddenly God, in his immense majesty, appeared to me and said to me: "He who has not seen me as little will not see me as great." And he added: "I have come and I have offered myself to you, now it is your turn to offer." But he did not say what or how or to whom I was supposed to offer myself. But immediately, my soul, in an indescribable and marvelous way, offered itself to him. Then I offered specifically and by name some of my sons. I offered myself and them perfectly and totally, withholding nothing for myself or for them. After this, I offered all my sons together. My soul perceived and understood that God accepted this offering and received it with great joy. I cannot describe the ineffable joy, delight, and sweetness I felt when I saw God receive and accept this offering with such kindness.

Instruction XXI

Jesus and Francis Come to Angela's Aid

Once when I lay sick in bed, I heard these words said by the suffering God-man: "Come to me you who are aglow with every agreeable color." And he added: "I want you to be my little martyr." [...] On another occasion during this same illness, while I lay in bed very weak and afflicted in body, the God-man Jesus appeared and consoled me very pleasantly. He began by showing me what is generally so pleasing to the sick, that is, a great compassion, with which, it seemed to me, he was greatly moved. Then he said to me: "I came here to serve you, and I want to serve you." The service he rendered to me was the following. He sat next to my bed and he was so pleasant to me that it is totally unspeakable. I can say absolutely nothing of the indescribable joy and delight that was mine to see and hear him. I saw him with the eyes of my soul far more clearly than the eyes of the body can see another body. This most clear and delightful vision bestowed on my soul a joy and a delight which is totally indescribable.

"You Are the Only One Born of Me"

After this, he showed me the blessed Francis and said: "Here is the one whom, after me, you have loved so much. I want him to serve you." Then the blessed Francis showed me the kinship and intimate love that was his for me, and it was great in every way. Great was my delight in the kinship and love which the blessed Francis demonstrated towards me. Afterwards, he spoke most secret and most high words to me. Finally, he said: "You are the only one born of me."

Instruction XXIII

"My Love for You Is Not a Hoax"

On Wednesday of Holy Week, I was meditating on the death of the Son of God incarnate; and trying to empty my soul of everything else so I could be more recollected in his passion and death. I had only one care, only one desire, and that was to find the best way to empty my soul from everything else in order to have a more vivid memory of the passion and death of the Son of God.

Suddenly, while I was engrossed in this effort and desire, a divine word sounded in my soul: "My love for you has not been a hoax." These words struck me a mortal blow. For immediately the eyes of my soul were opened and I saw that what he had said was true. I saw his acts of love, everything which the Son of God had done, all that he had endured in life and in death — this suffering God-man — because of his inexpressible and visceral love. Seeing in him all the deeds of true love, I understood the perfect truth of what he had said, that "his love for me had not been a hoax," but that he had loved me with a most perfect and visceral love. I saw, on the other hand, the exact opposite in myself, because my love for him had never been anything but playing games, never true. Being made aware of this was a mortal blow and caused such intolerable pain that I thought I would die.

Suddenly other words came to increase my sorrow. After he had said, "My love for you has not been a hoax" — and I had perceived that this was true on his part but quite the contrary on mine, and I had felt such pain that I thought I would die — he added: "I have not served you only in appearance" and then "I have not kept myself at a distance, but have always felt you close to me." These words increased my mortal pain and suffering even more. My soul cried out: "O Master, that which you assure me is not in you, is totally in me. My love for you has never been anything but a hoax and a lie. Nor have I ever really wanted to come close to you and feel the sufferings which you felt and endured for me. Furthermore, I have never served you, except in appearance and not truly." I perceived all the signs and marks of the truest love in him; how he had given himself wholly and totally to me, in order to serve me; how he had come so close to me: he had become human in order to truly feel and carry my sufferings in himself. When, on the other hand, I perceived the exact opposite in me, I had such suffering and pain that I thought I would die. I felt my ribs dislocate in my chest under the weight of my pain, and it seemed as though my heart would burst.[...] While I was thinking especially about the words he had said, "I have not kept myself at a distance, but have always felt you close to me," he added, "I am deeper within your soul than your soul is to itself." These words increased my suffering even more, because the more I perceived how deeply present he was to my soul, the more I knew that, for my part, I was far from him.

Afterwards, he added other words demonstrative of his deeply felt love. He said: "I would not withdraw my presence from anyone who wants to feel my presence deeply. It would also give me the greatest pleasure to grant a sight of me to anyone who wants to see me. I would likewise take great delight in speaking with anyone who wants to speak with me." These words stirred in my soul the desire not to feel, see, or say anything which could offend God. This is what God especially requires from his sons, because inasmuch as he called and chose them to feel his presence, see him, and speak with him, he wants them to be completely on their guard against everything to the contrary.

Instruction XXVIII

The Three Schools of Prayer

It is in prayer that one finds God. There are three schools, that is, three types of prayer, without which one does not find God. These are bodily, mental, and supernatural.

Bodily prayer takes place with the sound of words and bodily movements such as genuflections. I never abandon this type of prayer. For sometimes when I want to devote myself to mental prayer I am impeded by my laziness or by sleepiness. So I turn to bodily prayer, which leads to mental prayer. It should be done with attention. For instance, when you say the Our Father, you should weigh carefully what you are saying. Do not run through it, trying to complete a certain number of them, like little ladies doing piece work.

Prayer is mental when meditating on God so occupies the soul that one thinks of nothing but God. If some other thought comes to mind I no longer call such prayers mental. Such prayer curbs the tongue and renders one speechless. The mind is so totally filled with God's presence that it cannot think or speak about anything except about God and in God. From mental prayer, then, we move on to supernatural prayer. I call prayer supernatural when God, bestowing this gift upon the soul and filling it with his presence, so elevates the soul that it is stretched, as it were, beyond its natural capacities. In this type of prayer, the soul understands more of God than would seem naturally possible. It knows that it cannot understand, and what it knows it cannot explain, because all that it sees and feels is beyond its own nature. In these three schools of prayer you come to know who you are and who God is. From the fact that you know, you love. Loving, you desire to possess what you love. And this is the sign of true love: that the one who loves is transformed, not partially, but totally, into the Beloved. But because this transformation does not go on without interruption, the soul is seized by the desire to seek all the ways by which it can be transformed into the will of the Beloved, so it can return again to that vision. It seeks what was loved by the Beloved. God the Father provided a way for us to attain this transformation and this way is through the Beloved, that is, through God's own Son, whom he made the Son of poverty, suffering, contempt, and true obedience.

Instruction XXXVI

The Usefulness of Consolations

On another occasion Angela began to speak as follows: God in his overflowing love for the soul grants it caresses, that is, consolations, feelings of his presence, and other similar favors which I also call caresses. The soul should not seek these. But neither should it spurn them, because they make the soul speed along to God and are its food. It is as a result of these consolations that the soul makes its ascent in the love of God and strives to be transformed into the beloved.

Instruction XXXI

Angela's Last Words

These were the last words uttered by Angela of Foligno, the legitimate spouse of Christ, as she neared her happy passage from this life. First of all, at the beginning of her illness, on the feast of the Angels in September, Angela said: I wanted very much to receive communion on this feast of the Angels, but there was no one available to bring me the most sacred body of Christ. I became very sad. Then in the midst of this sadness and this desire to receive communion, I began to think about this feast and the praise of the angels, that is, their function and activity of praising God.

A Multitude of Angels

Suddenly, my soul was elevated and a great multitude of angels appeared to me. They led my soul to an altar and told me: "Here is the altar of the angels." On the altar they showed my soul the praise of the angels, that is, the one whom they praise and who is the praise of all. The angels then said to my soul: "In the one who is on the altar is the perfection and fulfillment of the sacrifice which you are seeking." And they added: "Prepare yourself to receive the one who has espoused you with the ring of his love. This union with him has already been realized. Now, he wishes to renew it." My soul truly experienced all this, and it was much more than words could express. These are but a shadow of what I experienced; my memory of it is only a shadow of the truth my soul experienced. But that shadow gladdens my soul more than I can say.

Every Creature Is Found Wanting

After this, while Angela lay shattered by her last illness, her mind was more than usually immersed and absorbed in the abyss of the divine infinity. She spoke only at intervals, a few brief phrases at a time, and rarely. We, who were present, tried to grasp what she said as best we could. We have briefly assembled her words as follows. Once, near the feast of the Nativity of Our Lord, at about the time she passed away to Christ, she said: "The Word was made flesh!" And, after a long delay, as if coming from another world, she added: "Oh, every creature is found wanting! Oh, the intelligence of the angels is likewise not enough!" We asked her: "How are creatures found wanting, and for what is the intelligence of angels not enough?" She responded: "To comprehend!"

The Storms That Assail the Soul

Afterwards, she said: "Behold, the moment has arrived in which my God fulfills his promise to me. Christ, his Son, has now presented me to the Father." But before this she had also said: "You know how when Christ was in the boat, there were great storms? Truly, it is some times like that with the soul. He permits storms to assail it, and he seems to sleep." And another time, she said: "In truth, God at times allows a person to be completely broken and downtrodden before he puts an end to the storm. He behaves in this way especially with his legitimate sons."

Final Words of Advice

On another occasion, she said: "My sons, I would be glad to tell you some things if I knew that God would not deceive me." She was referring to the promise of her approaching death, because having a great desire to die, as she said, she feared very much that God would restore her to health. Then she said: "What I wish to say, I say to you only in order that you might put into practice what I myself did not. I say it only for the honor of God and for your own profit. I do not want to take to the grave something that could be of help to you."Here is what God told my soul: "Whatever is mine is yours, and whatever is yours is mine." Who can deserve that all the riches of God should belong to her, that our riches should be God's and his ours? In truth nothing can deserve this except charity! O my dear little sons, fathers, and brothers, strive to love one another and to truly possess divine charity. Because by this charity and mutual love the soul deserves to inherit divine riches. I do not make any other testament except that I wish for you to have love for one another, and I leave you all that I have inherited: the life of Christ, that is, his poverty, suffering, and contempt.

Final Blessing

She placed her hand on the head of each of us saying: May God bless you, as I do, my dear sons, you and all the others who are not here. As Christ has showed to me an eternal blessing and indicated its meaning to me, so do I bestow that blessing, with all my heart, on you, both present and absent. And may Christ himself bestow it to you with that hand which was nailed on the cross. Those who will possess this inheritance, namely, the life of Christ and become true sons of prayer, will without doubt later possess the heritage of eternal life. Afterwards she added: My little children, strive to be charitable towards everyone, because I say to you that my soul truly received more from God when I wept and suffered with all my heart over the sins of others than when I wept over my own sins. Truly, there is no greater charity on earth than to suffer for the sins of others. The world could mock what I say, because it seems to be contrary to nature that someone could suffer and weep over the sins of one's neighbor more than for one's own. But the charity which does this is not of this world. My children, strive to have this charity.

Judge no one, even when you see someone commit mortal sin. I do not tell you that sin should not displease you, or that you should not abhor sin, but I say that you should not judge sinners, because you do not know the judgments of God. For many seem to us to be saved and are actually damned before God, and there are many who seem to us to be damned and are saved by God. I can tell you that there are some whom you have despised, who stray, that is, who are destroying the good things they have begun, but about whom I entertain a strong hope that God will lead them back to his way.

On another occasion, Angela said that her soul had been washed, cleansed and immersed in the blood of Christ, which was fresh and warm as if it flowed from the body of Christ on the cross. Then it was said to my soul: "This is what cleansed you." And my soul replied: "My God, will I be deceived?" "No," she was told.

The Robe of the Bride

My soul then heard these words: "O my spouse, my beautiful one, I love you with great affection. I do not want you to come to me burdened with these pains and sorrows, but jubilant and filled with ineffable joy. For it is only fitting for a king to wed his long-loved bride, clothed in royal garments." He showed me the robe which the bridegroom shows to the bride he has loved for so long. This robe was neither of purple, nor of scarlet, nor of sendal, nor of samite but of some marvelous light which clothed her soul.

The Manifestation of the Word

Then God showed me the Word, so that now I would understand what is meant by the Word and what it is to speak the Word. And he said to me: "This is the Word who wished to incarnate himself for you." At that very moment the Word came to me and went all through me, touched all of me, and embraced me.

Christ Comes in Person to Receive Angela

Before this, he had also said: "Come to me, my beloved, my beautiful one, my dearest, whom I love so much. Come, for all the saints are waiting for you with great joy." And he added: "I do not entrust to either the angels or any other saints the task of bringing you to me. I will come for you in person and I will take you with me." A long time before this he had also said:

"You have become suitable to be with me and have attained a most high place before my majesty." On another occasion she said: Cursed be the advantages in life which inflate the soul: power, honor, and ecclesiastical office! My little children, strive to be small.

O Unknown Nothingness!

And then she cried out: O unknown nothingness! O unknown nothingness! Truly, a soul cannot have a better awareness in this world than to perceive its own nothingness and to stay in its own cell. There is greater deception in spiritual advantages than in temporal ones — that is, to know how to speak about God, to do great penances, to understand the Scriptures, and to have one's heart almost constantly preoccupied with spiritual matters. For those who are taken by them fall many times into errors and are more difficult to lead back to the right way than those who have temporal advantages. And again she cried out: O unknown nothingness! When she was near death, the very day before she died, she frequently said: "Father, into your hands I commend my soul and my spirit." One time, after she said this, she told us: "I have just received this answer to what I said: that which is imprinted on your heart in life, it is impossible not to have in death." Then we asked her: "Do you want to go away and leave us?" She replied: "I have kept it hidden from you, but now no longer. I must go."

The Promised State of Jubilation

That very day, all her suffering ceased. For many days before she had been horribly tormented and afflicted in every single part of herself, internally and externally. But now her body lay in such a state of rest and her soul in such happiness that she seemed to taste already some of the joy promised to her. We asked her then if this promised state of jubilation had indeed been granted to her. And she responded that, true enough, she was already in this said joy-filled state. She remained lying with her body and mind at rest and in a jubilant mood until Saturday night after compline. She was surrounded by many friars who celebrated the Divine Office in her presence. It was during the last hour of that day, on the octave of the Feast of the Holy Innocents that, as if gently falling asleep, she died peacefully. Thus, her most holy soul, freed from the flesh and absorbed into the abyss of divine charity, received from Christ, her spouse, the stole of immortality and innocence to reign with him forever. Where she is, may we too be led by the power of the most holy cross, the merits of Christ's most holy mother, and the intercession of our most holy mother, Angela, by Jesus Christ himself, the Son of God, who lives and reigns with the Father and the Holy Spirit, forever and ever. Amen.

Obituary

The venerable spouse of Christ, Angela of Foligno, passed from the shipwreck of this world into the joys of heaven — promised to her a long time before — in the year of our Lord 1309, January 4, during the reign of Pope Clement V. Thanks be to God. Amen.

Epilogue

(Penned by one of Angela's disciples, a Franciscan Spiritual)

[...] [Angela] is truly a shining light of God, a mirror without blemish of God's majesty, and an image of his goodness. Although she is only one person she can do all things. Even though she remains in herself, she renews all and her influence extends itself to holy souls throughout the world. She makes all her sons prophets of truth and friends of God. Truly, anyone who fights against Angela — or rather, against the way of Christ, and his life, and his teachings — has no love for anyone.... It is not against the order of providence that God, to men's shame, made a woman a teacher — and one that to my knowledge has no match on earth...

Chronology

Angela of Foligno (1248-1309)

Birth in Foligno, a small Umbrian town not far from Assisi. Well-to-do; married with sons; shares conventional aspirations of her times.

The Memorial

Prologue
The purpose of this book is to demonstrate the possibility of becoming aware of the presence of the Trinity in oneself as proven by the experience and the teachings of "a certain faithful follower of Christ" (Angela).

The First Twenty Steps (1285-1291 ca.)

Conversion 1285, 37 (ca.) years old. Awareness of a wasted life.

Time of painful struggle and effort (steps 1-9).
1. Awareness of one's sinfulness in which the soul greatly fears being damned to hell; it also receives the grace to weep from shame and bitterness.

2. St. Francis appears to Angela in the form of an elderly friar to help her find a good confessor. She makes a full confession to him, but is still grief-stricken.
3. The soul performs unspecified penance in satisfaction to God.

4. Growing awareness of divine mercy.

5. Knowledge of self and of one's defects.

6. Soul is illumined to see how it has offended others, begs for and is granted their forgiveness.

7. Receives the grace to look at the Cross but it is without savor and causes grief.

8. Greater perception of the meaning of the Cross which sets Angela so on fire that she strips herself of all her clothing; accuses herself for sins committed by each member of her body; gives herself totally to Christ and promises perpetual chastity.

9. Begins to seek the way of the cross by forgiving everyone who had offended her, strips herself of everything worldly, all attachments to everyone, all her possessions and even her very self. Mother, husband and sons die and she experiences it as a great consolation. Her heart is now in God's heart and God's heart in hers.

10. Christ crucified appears to her, shows her each of his wounds and how he endured them for her.

11. Angela performs ever harsher unspecified penance.

12. Resolves to become poor and overcomes the fear and shame of begging in spite of advice to the contrary.

13. Enters into the sorrow over the Passion suffered by Mary and John. Christ shows her his heart.

14. While in prayer Christ calls Angela to place her mouth to the wound at his side, which inspires her to desire a death as cruel and as vile as possible.

15. Fixes her attention on John and Mary and their sorrow at the foot of the cross which inspires Angela to dispose of her belongings even more radically. She is still in a state of bitter sorrow.

16. Begins to taste something of God's sweetness while reciting the Our Father.

17. Enters into mystical consciousness, " a state different from before" by recollecting herself in the passion of Christ. Experiences ecstasy while meditating on a Scripture passage.

18. So afire with the love of God that Angela falls feverish and sick whenever she sees depictions of the Passion.

19. First great sensation of God's sweetness while contemplating the divinity and humanity of Christ. Now finds satisfaction only in God. Receives the promise that the Holy Trinity will come into her.

20. While on pilgrimage to Assisi, Angela is overwhelmed by a numinous experience of divine intimacy.

Supplementary Steps (1291-1296)

First Supplementary Step
Further description of her pilgrimage to Assisi. Experience of the Holy Spirit. Swooning episode in front of the stained glass window depicting St. Francis being held closely by Christ in the Basilica of St. Francis in Assisi. Espousal with Christ.

Vision of a shining star radiating from her body. Removal of doubt that the Trinity had entered into her. Visions of the beauty of Christ's throat and body on the cross likened to those experienced during the Eucharist.

Second Supplementary Step
Immense joy experienced from the unction of God's presence embracing her and thrilling her body with delight. Asks for a sign and receives the promise of feeling God's presence continually and burning with love for him. Discovery that God is the love of the soul and wants nothing other save love in return. Begins to experience formless visions such as the indescribable beauty of God. Need to show oneself to Christ the divine doctor and follow his orders to be restored to health. Certitude of God's presence which sets the soul ablaze especially during the celebration of the Eucharist.

Third Supplementary Step
Teachings (the way of tribulation) concerning the legitimate sons of God invited to eat at the same plate and drink at the same cup as the Lord at his banquet. As an example of the power of God to transform suffering into sweetness, Angela and her companion drink the water used to wash the festering wounds of a leper and experiences it as sweet as receiving Holy Communion. More formless visions.

Fourth Supplementary Step
Made aware of her unworthiness, tempted by the devil, liberated and elevated to a new state. Vision of the world "as pregnant with God." Learns how God plays with the soul. Experiences Christ embracing her soul with the very arm with which he was crucified. Miraculously drawn into a state of delight at the sight of a Passion play. Formless visions of the will and power of God and as the All Good.

Fifth Supplementary Step

Sees the poverty of Christ, even as poor of himself and powerless to help himself. Perceives more of the Passion of Christ than she has ever heard spoken of. Receives the grace of being united with God's will. In a state of ecstasy has a vision of herself united with Christ in the sepulcher. Experience of God's love approaching her and moving like a sickle. Vision of the Blessed Virgin and Christ in glory. While receiving communion experiences a formless vision of God as the All Good and at another moment the savor of the host in her mouth. The seven ways in which God comes into the soul, in particular the experience of the Pilgrim. Visible effects of the presence of God within her. Attains simultaneously a knowledge of self and the goodness of God.

Sixth Supplementary Step

Horrible torments of body and soul. Sharing in Christ's abandonment on the Cross. Terrible darkness unknown before. Struggle with pride and a certain type of humility. How this struggle purifies the soul.

Seventh Supplementary Step

The most wonderful step of all. In a new way sees the light, the beauty, and the fullness that is in God: loses the love that was hers and becomes non-love. Sees God in and with darkness. Drawn by the darkness into the depths of the Trinitarian life and sees the God-man who tells her: "You are I and I am You." No longer any intermediary between God and herself. Cross becomes her bed to rest on. Perceives the wisdom and depths of divine judgments. Drawn out of everything experienced before into deeper and even more ineffable workings of the Trinity. In one manner God manifests himself in the intimacy of her soul so that she understands how he is present in an angel and in a devil in good as well as in evil actions. In another manner, God manifests by totally recollecting her in himself.

Words blaspheme for none can be found to explain this deeper awareness of God's presence. The mysteries of the Holy Scriptures are revealed. Becomes aware of a chamber in the soul where no joy or sadness can enter. The soul experiences its own presentation which it cannot comprehend yet this experience is accompanied by even greater delights and the awareness that nothing can separate her from God. This experience, though different, is the same that the saints enjoy in eternal life. God puts the seal on the veracity of everything that has been written.

The Instructions (dates of composition ca. 1297-1318)

Instruction II
The Weapons to Protect True Love
The Pitfalls of Love
The Love that is Perfect

Instruction III
The Necessity of Prayer
Warnings against the False Teachers of Prayer
The Purpose of Prayer: Manifestation of God and Self
Three Modalities of Prayer
The Highest Levels of Prayer
Poverty. Teachings of the Blessed Francis

Instruction VII
Advice for Those Involved in Pastoral Ministry

Instruction IX
Advice on Avoiding Divisions

Instruction XIV
Knowledge of God and Knowledge of Self

Instruction XV
To be Perfect in the Ways of God: Run to the Cross

Instruction XVII
Birth of the Child Jesus in the Soul

Instruction XVIII
The Necessity of Persevering in Prayer
The Smile of Friendship

Instruction XIV
Vision on the Feast of the Purification of Mary
Offering of Herself and her Spiritual Sons

Instruction XXI
Christ Consoles Angela in her Sickness
St. Francis Tells Angela: "You are the Only One Born of Me"

Instruction XXIII
"My Love for You Has Not Been a Hoax"

Instruction XXVIII
The Three Schools of Prayer

Instruction XXXI
The Usefulness of Consolations

Instruction XXXVI
Angela's Last Words

Death: Jan. 4, 1309.

Beatification: July 11, 1701.

ALSO AVAILABLE IN THE SAME SERIES FROM NEW CITY PRESS

AELRED OF RIEVAULX—THE WAY OF FRIENDSHIP
M. BASIL PENNINGTON (ed.)
ISBN 1-56548-128-3-0, paper, 168 pp.

BERNARD OF CLAIRVAUX—A LOVER TEACHING THE WAY OF LOVE
M. BASIL PENNINGTON (ed.)
ISBN 1-56548-089-9, 3d printing, paper, 128 pp.

CATHERINE OF SIENA—PASSION FOR THE TRUTH . . .
MARY O'DRISCOLL, O.P. (ed.)
ISBN 1-56548-235-2, 7th printing, paper, 144 pp.

FRANCIS DE SALES—FINDING GOD WHEREVER YOU ARE
JOSEPH F. POWER, O.S.F.S. (ed.)
ISBN 1-56548-074-0, 5th printing, paper, 160 pp.

JOHN HENRY NEWMAN—HEART SPEAKS TO HEART
LAWRENCE S. CUNNINGHAM (ed.)
ISBN 1-56548-193-3, paper, 128 pp.

JOHN OF THE CROSS—THE ASCENT TO JOY
MARC FOLEY, O.C.D. (ed.)
ISBN 1-56548-174-7, paper, 152 pp.

JULIAN OF NORWICH—JOURNEYS INTO JOY
JOHN NELSON (ed.)
ISBN 1-56548-134-8, 2d printing, paper, 184 pp.

MARTIN LUTHER—FAITH IN CHRIST AND THE GOSPEL
ERIC W. GRITSCH (ed.)
ISBN 1-56548-041-4, 2d printing, paper, 192 pp.

MEDIEVAL WOMEN MYSTICS—Gertrude the Great, Angela of Foligno, Birgitta of Sweden, Julian of Norwich
ELIZABETH RUTH OBBARD (ed.)
ISBN 1-56548-157-7, 2d printing, paper, 168 pp.

SAINT BENEDICT—A RULE FOR BEGINNERS
JULIAN STEAD, O.S.B. (ed.)
ISBN 1-56548-057-0, 5th printing, paper, 160 pp.